D1517144

NEW YORK

THEN AND NOW®

First published in the United Kingdom in 2015 by
PAVILION BOOKS
an imprint of Pavilion Books Company Ltd.
1 Gower Street, London WC1E 6HD, UK

"Then and Now" is a registered trademark of
Salamander Books Limited,
a division of Pavilion Books Group.

© 2015 Salamander Books Limited, a division of Pavilion Books Group.

This book is a revision of the original compact edition of *New York
Then and Now* first produced in 2013 by Salamander Books, a division
of Pavilion Books Group.

Copyright under International, Pan American, and Universal Copyright
Conventions. All rights reserved. No part of this book may be
reproduced or transmitted in any form or by any means, electronic or
mechanical, including photocopying, recording, or by any information
storage-and-retrieval system, without written permission from the
copyright holder. Brief passages (not to exceed 1,000 words) may be
quoted for reviews.

All notations of errors or omissions should be addressed to
Salamander Books, 1 Gower Street, London WC1E 6HD, UK.

ISBN-13: 978-1-91090-413-8

Printed in China

10 9 8 7 6 5 4 3 2 1

Author's Acknowledgments
To my husband, Charles Reiss, who can identify nearly every New York
building and helped me peel away the layers of history in the city's
skyline. Thanks also to Evan Joseph for his amazing skill and energy
in getting the best photos, and to Senior Editor David Salmo for
putting it all together.

Photographer's Acknowledgments
This book is dedicated with love to my beautiful wife Amy, a fellow
artist who understands perfectly that getting it right is worth
whatever it takes. To my talented collaborators, writer Marcia Reiss
and editor David Salmo, thank you for always being willing to find
another Then to match a better Now. And I would like to gratefully
acknowledge the assistance of my wonderful clients, who shared
their enthusiasm and knowledge of New York City and got me into
some unusual places to take these photos.

Bibliography
Jackson, Kenneth T., editor, *The Encyclopedia of New York City*,
    Yale University Press, New Haven, 1995.
Stern, Robert A. M. and others, *New York: 1880; New York: 1960*,
    The Monacelli Press, New York, 1999, 1997.
Stern, Robert A. M. and others, *New York: 1900; New York: 1930*,
    Rizzoli International Publications, Inc., New York, 1983, 1987.
White, Norval, and Willensky, Elliot, with Fran Leadon, *AIA Guide to
    New York City*, Oxford University Press, New York, 2010.

Picture Credits
All "Then" photographs are courtesy of the Library of Congress,
except for the following: Corbis (8, 14 main, 16, 18 main, 21, 22, 27, 30
right, 38, 72 right, 116, 118, 128 main); Getty Images (10, 36 main, 39
bottom, 48–49, 70, 96, 104, 107, 123, 136 right, 141); New York Historical
Society (34 main, 80, 94 bottom, 100 bottom, 106, 112); Pavilion Image
Library (36 right, 66, 90, 110, 119); Mary Evans Picture Library (59); Jim
Shaughnessy (67); ElectroSpark (140, 142, 143).

"Now" photographs:
All "Now" photographs by Evan Joseph (@evanjosephphoto).

NEW YORK
THEN AND NOW®

MARCIA REISS

"NOW" PHOTOGRAPHY
BY EVAN JOSEPH

PAVILION

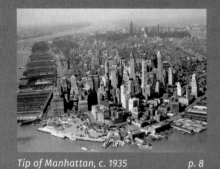
Tip of Manhattan, c. 1935   p. 8

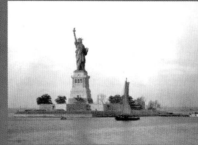
Statue of Liberty, 1890   p. 14

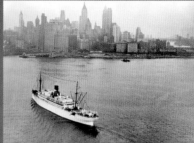

Lower Manhattan Skyline, 1934   p. 20

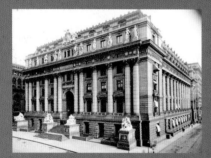
U.S. Custom House, 1915   p. 22

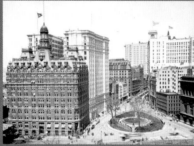
Bowling Green, 1900   p. 24

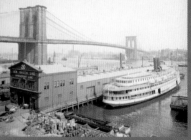
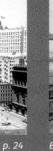
Brooklyn Bridge, 1905   p. 50

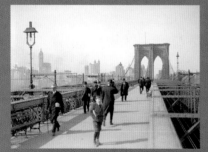
Brooklyn Bridge Walkway, c. 1920   p. 52

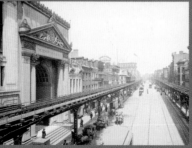
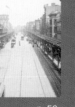
Bowery Savings Bank, c. 1905   p. 58

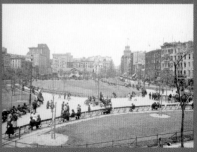
Mulberry Bend, 1905   p. 62

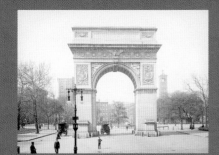

Washington Square Arch, 1905   p. 68

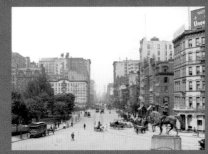

Union Square East, c. 1905   p. 74

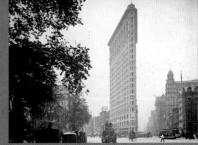

Flatiron Building, c. 1905   p. 82

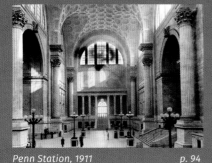

Penn Station, 1911   p. 94

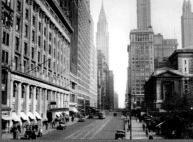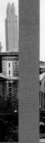

Forty-second Street, c. 1935   p. 104

Times Tower, 1908   p. 108

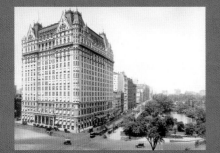

Plaza Hotel, c. 1910   p. 124

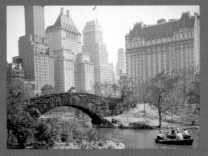

Gapstow Bridge, Central Park, 1933   p. 128

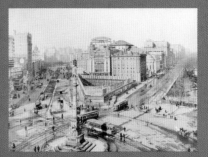

Columbus Circle, 1912   p. 134

New York City has seen more than a decade of dramatic changes since the first edition of *New York Then and Now* was published in 2000. The most dramatic, of course, came just a year later in the terrorist attack on the World Trade Center towers in 2001—the greatest tragedy in New York's history and the most sudden and shocking alteration of the city's landscape. Although nothing can replace the loss of so many lives, the city returned to near normality only a few years later. But for New York City, normality is a state of constant change. Since the loss of the Twin Towers, the island of Manhattan has continued to transform itself, as it has done since its founding four centuries ago, from a Dutch village to America's most densely packed urban environment.

Even after the economic downturn in 2008, Manhattan has continued to build and rebuild itself. The devastation of Ground Zero became a hive of construction, and the first new tower, One World Trade Center, is the city's tallest structure. But the changes are not just a matter of new buildings. The city is also experiencing the transformation of entire neighborhoods from industrial and commercial to residential use. Throughout the nineteenth century, this change took place in reverse, as fashionable families moved their homes uptown, escaping the intrusion of business and traffic. But recently the pendulum has been swinging back from commercial to residential development. Even more unusual, it is happening in the same buildings, as office towers, factories, and warehouses are converted to condos and lofts.

The trend started in the 1960s in SoHo, spread to Tribeca and Wall Street in the 1980s, and is now taking place throughout the downtown area, creating distinct new residential neighborhoods, like the Flatiron District, named for the triangular tower built in 1903. Most recently—and most surprisingly—the trend is also taking place in Lower Manhattan around the World Trade Center site. After the terror and heartbreak of September 11, New Yorkers have been returning to work and live in converted office towers only a short walk from Ground Zero. At the same time, new buildings have risen in the area, notably the shimmering

NEW YORK
THEN AND NOW INTRODUCTION

steel tower near the Brooklyn Bridge, designed by the acclaimed architect Frank Gehry. At seventy-six stories, it is one of the tallest residential buildings in the city.

This edition of *New York Then and Now*, places today's cityscape within the context of history, reflecting the changing and enduring aspects of life in New York. The historic photos reveal the many ways New Yorkers lived, worked and moved about the city, how they entertained themselves, followed the latest fashions, celebrated great events, and endured hardship and even tragedy more than a century ago. The chaotic scene of the Wall Street bombing of 1920 now looks like a somber precursor to September 11. Together with the appearance of luxury condos on the same Wall Street corner, it also reveals New York's amazing resilience.

The city advanced through a series of prodigious achievements. In 1842, the Croton Aqueduct brought clean drinking water from an upstate source to a massive reservoir in the middle of Manhattan, greatly improving the health of its citizens. Central Park, St. Patrick's Cathedral, and Grand Central Station expanded the city northward, shaping its raw edge into elegant neighborhoods and thriving business districts. Many incredible undertakings progressed in the midst of earth-shaking events. Progress on Central Park and St. Patrick's Cathedral was interrupted, but not derailed, by the Civil War. Rockefeller Center, the city's largest private real estate venture, was built during the worst years of the Depression. Some of the biggest projects were built simultaneously: Penn Station, Grand Central Terminal, the New York Public Library, the Manhattan Bridge, and the Woolworth Building, the world's tallest in its day, were all completed by 1913. The Empire State Building and the George Washington Bridge both opened in 1931.

As the city changed its appearance, so did its population. From 1855 to 1924, twenty million people passed through New York's immigration centers, first at Castle Clinton and then at Ellis Island. Although they settled in many parts of the country, millions stayed in the city, forever changing the face and culture of its neighborhoods. Their diverse and energetic activities are reflected in the photos of St. Patrick's Cathedral, built with the hard-earned donations of Irish immigrants; in the Mulberry Street market of Little Italy; the Columbus Circle monument, erected by Italian Americans; and Temple Emanu-El, built by German Jews on the Fifth Avenue site formerly occupied by a Gilded Age mansion.

New York's signature skyscrapers flourished in Lower Manhattan through the first decades of the twentieth century. Vertical buildings were an efficient way to build office space on these narrow streets. But as tower after tower rose in Midtown—Manhattan's widest point—it became increasingly clear that efficiency was not the driving force. Prestige, pride, and power pushed corporations to aim for the sky. Architects envisioned a city of towers in splendid isolation, but layers of modern development now surround the most distinctive profiles within the skyline—the Chrysler and Empire State buildings.

The historic photos display many other extraordinary structures. Development of the elevator, telephone, and electric lighting in the late nineteenth century produced not only skyscrapers, but also palatial department stores and the largest and most lavish hotels in the city's history. Macy's, Wanamaker's, and Siegel-Cooper's (a name now known only by a plaque on the Bed, Bath and Beyond store on the old Ladies' Mile) were built to serve the rising middle class. The first Waldorf-Astoria, the Sherry-Netherland, and the famed Plaza Hotel became legendary meeting places for the rich and famous.

One of New York's magnificent buildings, Penn Station, was demolished in 1963 for a mundane replacement, an inconceivable act of destruction today. The loss led to the city's first landmark protection law that preserved Grand Central Station and many other great buildings within these pages. Today, New York is an astounding mix of old and new, an ever-changing picture of a dynamic city.

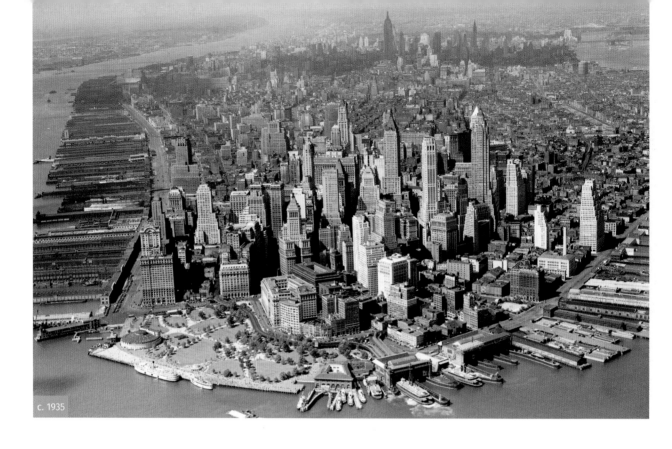

c. 1935

TIP OF MANHATTAN

A distinct and ever-changing cityscape

ABOVE: By the 1930s, the southern tip of Manhattan was a mass of skyscrapers. Standing shoulder to shoulder on a slender island, the towers seemed to defy their own stability. Fortunately, Manhattan's physical foundation was built on bedrock, unshakable schist formed hundreds of millions of years ago by intense heat and pressure. Yet the shoreline seen here is all man's doing. Ever since the Dutch settled Manhattan in the early seventeenth century, they began adding real estate by extending the waterfront with dirt and rocks. The swath of land that is now Battery Park, the piers reaching up the Hudson River (left of the city), and those along the East River (right) are all landfill extensions.

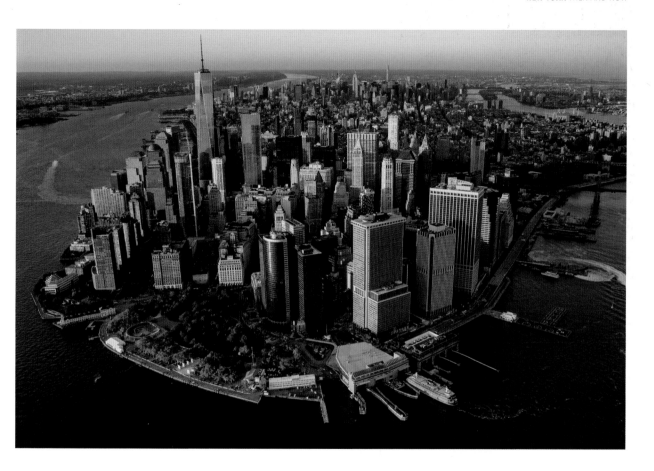

ABOVE: The World Trade Center towers reshaped this familiar cityscape in the early 1970s. After they fell in 2001, it seemed strangely empty. Now that One World Trade Center has reached its full height of 1,776 feet, Lower Manhattan once again has a distinctive high point. The waterfront has taken new shape with the rise of Battery Park City and the World Financial Center on the landfill created from the excavation of the Twin Towers, north of Battery Park (foreground). Once lined with ships, most of the old piers have been transformed into parks and other public facilities along the Hudson and East Rivers. But at least one thing on the waterfront is still the same: the orange Staten Island ferryboat was also running in the 1930s photo. The city began the service in 1905.

ELLIS ISLAND

The island grew to nearly ten times its original size to accommodate the swelling tide of immigration

BELOW: By the time of this 1930s photo, the Ellis Island immigration center was long past its peak. From 1892 to 1924, twelve million people were processed through these buildings. Henry James visited the center at the height of its operation in 1907, the single year in which more than a million people had entered. As he described in *The American Scene*, the arrivals had to undergo a long and tedious process of officially entering the United States: "they stand appealing and waiting, marshalled, herded, divided, subdivided, sorted, sifted, searched, fumigated." The immigration center, which moved from Castle Clinton to Ellis Island in 1892, at first occupied a series of wooden buildings. The entry process became a bit more humane when those were replaced by the Great Hall in 1900 and supporting facilities by 1906. The island itself was ultimately enlarged through landfill from three to twenty-seven acres.

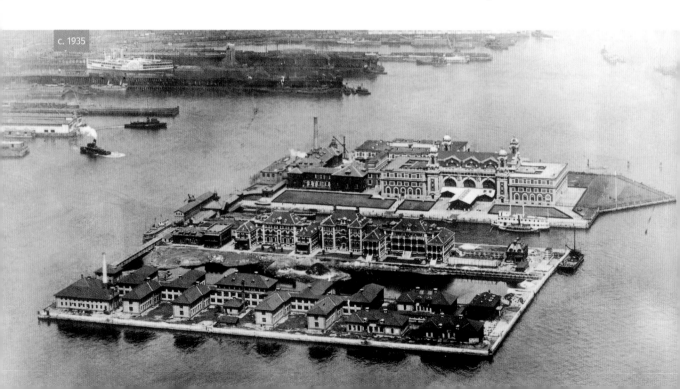

c. 1935

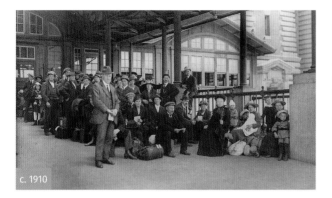

c. 1910

LEFT: New arrivals in the early 1900s await medical examinations, just one step in the long process of seeking entry to the United States.

BELOW: Strict quotas established in 1921 and 1924 severely limited the number of people who could enter the country. From 1925 to the facility's closing in 1954, only 2.3 million immigrants passed through Ellis Island—still more than half of all those entering the United States. After the immigration center closed, the buildings fell into ruins and the deterioration continued even after the island was declared a national monument in 1965. The Ellis Island Foundation, established in 1982, reopened the Great Hall as a museum in 1990. Many of the other buildings in the complex still await restoration. Today, more than forty percent of American citizens can trace their ancestors to arrivals at Ellis Island.

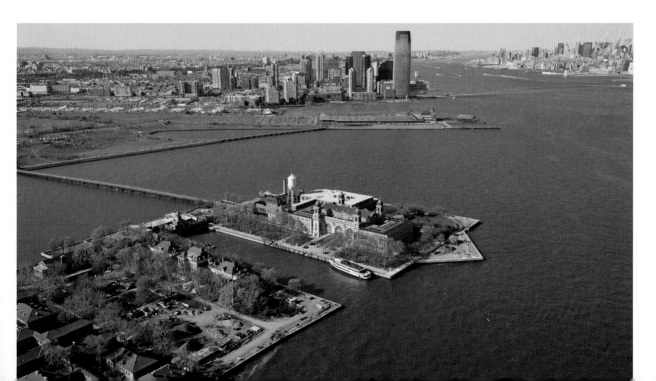

GOVERNORS ISLAND

Minutes from Manhattan, the island is currently being transformed from a military base to a public retreat

BELOW: A mere 800 yards away from Manhattan's Battery Park (foreground), Governors Island was the exclusive quarters of the royal governors who ruled New York during the colonial era. The most notorious was Lord Cornbury, who was removed from office in 1708 after the colonists complained that he was corrupt. The island became a U.S. Army base in 1783. Fort Jay in the center of the island and the circular Castle Williams, on the right shoreline, were built to keep the British at bay during the War of 1812. Shortly before this photo was taken in 1911, the island had more than doubled in size with landfill excavated for Manhattan's Lexington Avenue subway.

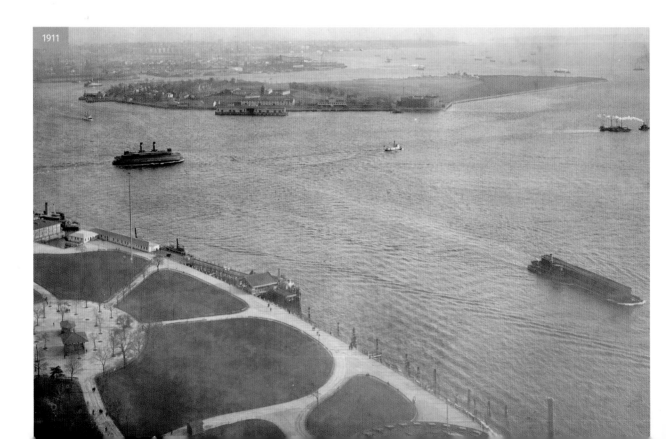

1911

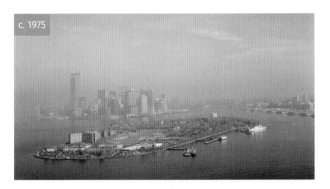

c. 1975

ABOVE: The foreground of this 1970s aerial view shows modern housing on the island's Coast Guard base. Lower Manhattan and the World Trade Center are on the left, and the Brooklyn waterfront is on the right.

BELOW: In 1966, the Coast Guard took over the island's army base and created a new town of 3,500 personnel. Thirty years later, the entire base was closed, leaving a well-preserved ghost town. After several years of public pressure, the federal government declared the two historic forts and the surrounding twenty-two acres a national monument. In 2003, it transferred the remaining 150 acres to the people of New York "to be used for public benefit." While real estate developers and park advocates debated the meaning of "public benefit," the agreement prohibited casinos and private housing, opening the door to the creation of a public park. In 2010, the city and state established the Trust for Governors Island, an organization now rebuilding the island's infrastructure and planning its future. In the meantime, the island, accessible by frequent ferries, is open for summer visits, and the public can enjoy its historic buildings and amazing views. The gray, boxy structure off the island's left shore is the air shaft for the Brooklyn-Battery Tunnel, which runs under the river. Castle Clinton, minus its roof, is in the foreground of Battery Park.

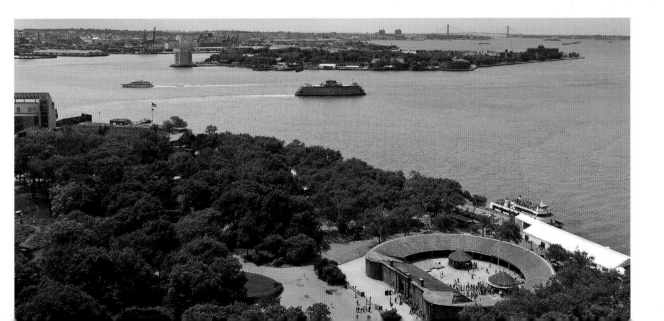

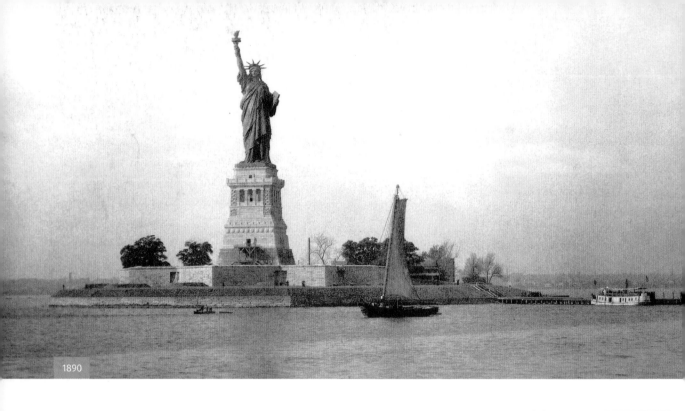
1890

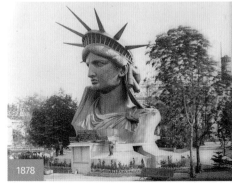
1878

STATUE OF LIBERTY

An American icon, created in France

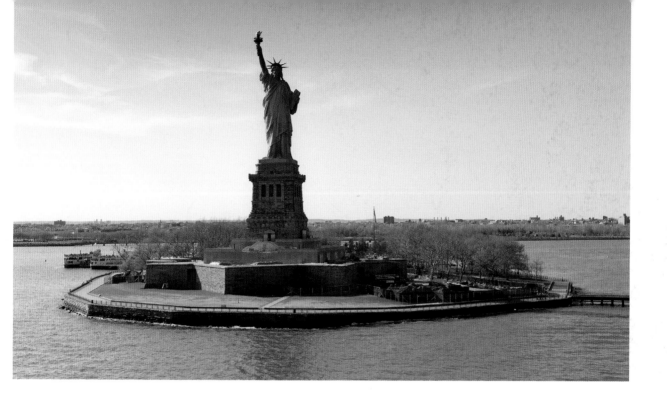

ABOVE LEFT: Titled "Liberty Enlightening the World," the Statue of Liberty had been proposed in France in 1865 during the reign of Napoléon III's repressive monarchy. The man behind the idea, Édouard de Laboulaye, a fervent abolitionist, wanted to celebrate both democratic freedom and the Union victory in the Civil War. The broken shackle and chain at the statue's feet symbolized the emancipation. Sculptor Frédéric Auguste Bartholdi designed the statue and Alexandre Gustave Eiffel, creator of the Eiffel Tower in 1889, engineered its steel skeleton. The colossal figure became a stirring symbol of welcome to millions of immigrants arriving in New York in the late nineteenth century. In 1903, a plaque was installed inside the pedestal, bearing the now famous lines by Emma Lazarus: "Give me your tired, your poor, your huddled masses yearning to breathe free."

ABOVE: The statue got a total makeover for its centennial on July 4, 1986. French artisans came to New York to work on the statue, as their countrymen had done a century before. Although it also commemorates the French-American alliance during the Revolutionary War, the statue is clearly an American icon, and the French connection is only a subtext today. Closed after the World Trade Center attacks on September 11, 2001, the Statue of Liberty did not reopen until August 2004. The monumental pedestal, as tall as the statue, has a glass ceiling that affords views into the figure. Visitors who can climb up the 354 steps inside the statue are able to see amazing views from inside her spiked crown.

FAR LEFT: Completed in 1878, Liberty's head was displayed in Paris eight years before the entire statue was erected in New York.

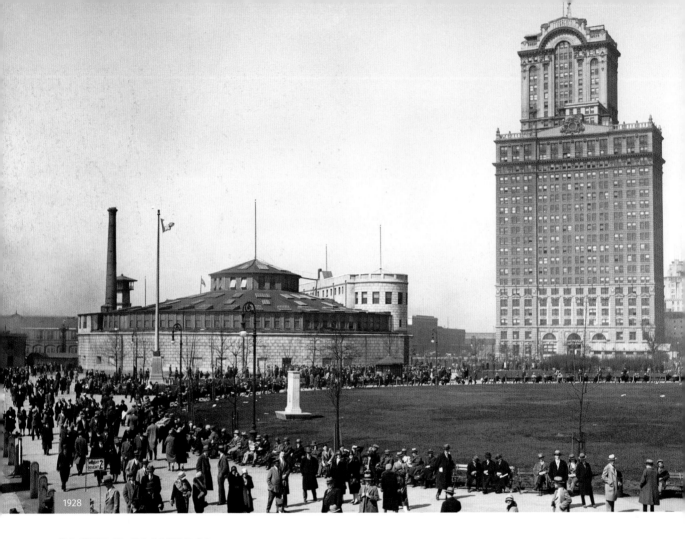

1928

CASTLE CLINTON

Nearly destroyed, the 200-year-old fort survived
as a national monument

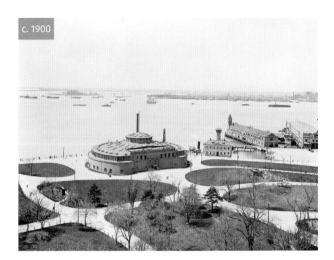

c. 1900

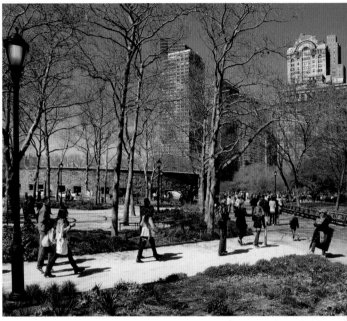

LEFT: The foreground of this photo was originally all water. The round Castle Clinton, built in 1811 and outfitted with a battery of twenty-eight cannons, stood on a rocky outcrop some 200 feet offshore. The waterfront was extended around it by landfill and eventually became Battery Park. Remodeled in 1823, the fort became a restaurant and concert hall, renamed Castle Garden. Along with opera and theatrical performances, many new inventions were demonstrated here, including the telegraph. In 1855, it became the Emigrant Landing Depot, processing eight million arrivals until 1892, the year Ellis Island took over the job. The castle found new life in 1896 as the city's aquarium, seen here in that role in 1928. The tall Whitehall Building is actually two buildings. The lower, rectangular one was built in 1904. The second, towering above it with an arched top, is a thirty-one-story addition, built in 1910.

ABOVE: In its heyday as an aquarium, Castle Clinton was the most popular public institution in the city.

ABOVE: Castle Clinton and all of Battery Park were nearly destroyed in the 1940s by a plan to build a bridge from this spot to Brooklyn. They were saved by a public outcry that transformed the project into the Brooklyn–Battery Tunnel, with excavation beginning under the park. Sadly, the old fort was stripped of its roof, the aquarium was dismantled, and the building was gutted down to its stone walls. At the last minute, it was spared from total destruction by a court ruling, preserving it as a national monument. It now serves as the place to buy tickets for excursions to the Statue of Liberty and receives three million visitors a year.

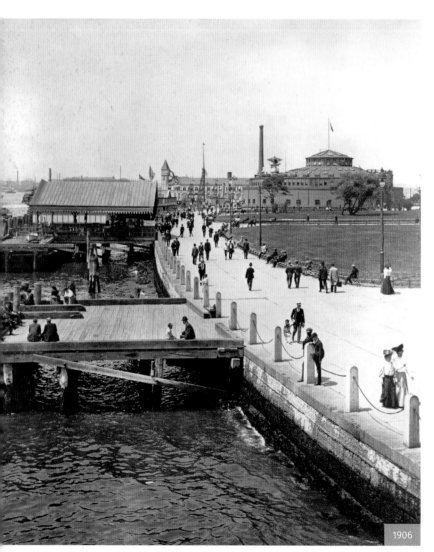

BATTERY PARK BOARDWALK

A popular promenade for more than two centuries

LEFT: Once fortified with a battery of guns, Manhattan's southern shoreline was used as a public promenade as early as 1790. By the time of this 1906 photo, it had been reshaped into a formal esplanade bordering the manicured lawns of Battery Park. Castle Clinton, the round building in the far right background, was operating at this time as the New York Aquarium. The structure immediately to its left is Pier A, a long, covered dock with a peaked tower at the end. Built in 1886, it was New York's formal reception pier, where city officials greeted important visitors arriving by ship.

BELOW: An aerial view of Battery Park and Lower Manhattan in the 1920s.

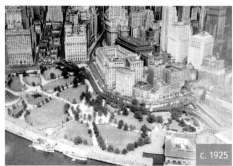

c. 1925

RIGHT: The boardwalk was officially named the Admiral Dewey Promenade in 1973, the seventy-fifth anniversary of Dewey's victory in the Spanish–American War. Today, the view takes in towering buildings on both sides of the harbor. Castle Clinton, obscured by trees, is the place to buy tickets to the Statue of Liberty and Ellis Island, and the ferry to these harbor sites approaches the tents on the boardwalk where passengers wait to board the boat. The two rows of concrete slabs in the park are engraved with the names of more than 4,600 U.S. servicemen lost during World War II in the Atlantic Ocean. After years of neglect, all of Battery Park, the historic site of the Dutch settlement of New Amsterdam, is sprouting beautiful gardens created by the Dutch landscape designer Piet Oudolf. The landmarked but long-vacant Pier A was restored and reopened as a three-story restaurant complex in 2014.

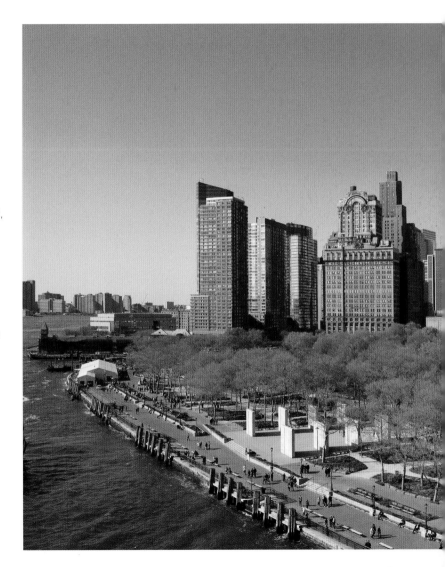

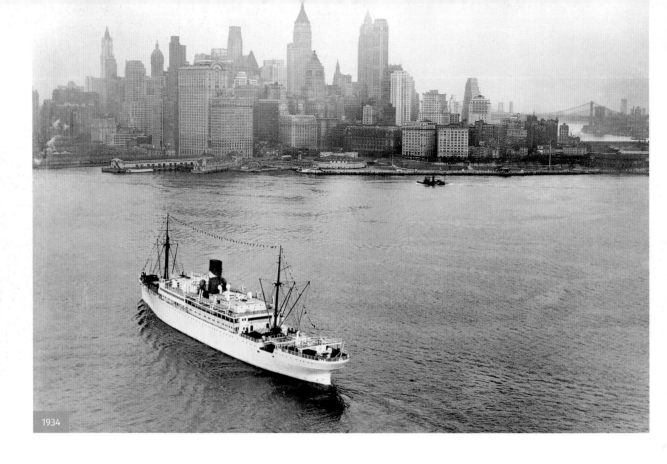

1934

LOWER MANHATTAN SKYLINE

Skyscrapers became the signature of the New York skyline in the early twentieth century

ABOVE: Despite the Great Depression, New York in 1934 still presented an impressive skyline to new arrivals. The spires of several famous skyscrapers stand out. On the left is the Woolworth Building (1913) and the Singer Building with its curved crown (1909). In the center, the seventy-one-story Bank of Manhattan Building (1930) is the tallest structure in Lower Manhattan. To the far right are the overlapping towers of three spans over the East River: the Brooklyn, Manhattan, and Williamsburg Bridges. Castle Clinton, the low circular building along the shoreline, also can be seen in Battery Park.

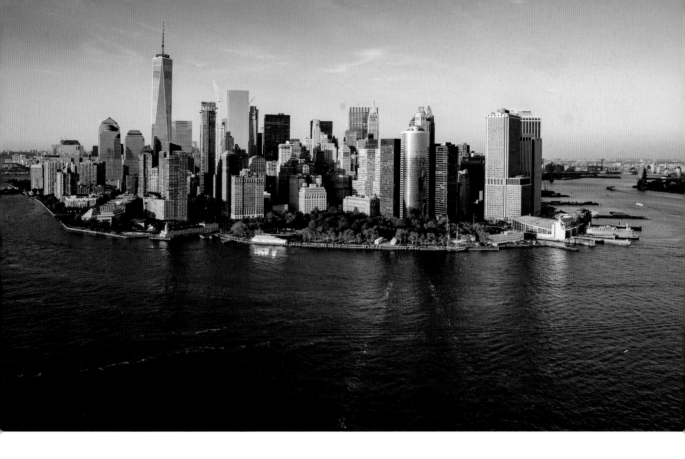

ABOVE: Much bigger and bulkier than in 1934, the skyline has been totally reshaped by development, new architectural styles, and tragic events. The skyline's former peak, the World Trade Center towers (shown in the photo on the right), is gone, but the new One World Trade Center, which reaches 1,776 feet (top left), was completed on the site in 2014. The former Bank of America Building is still visible with its turquoise peak, just right of center, but a wall of later office towers obscures most of the earlier skyscrapers.

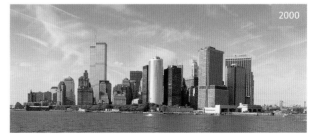

2000

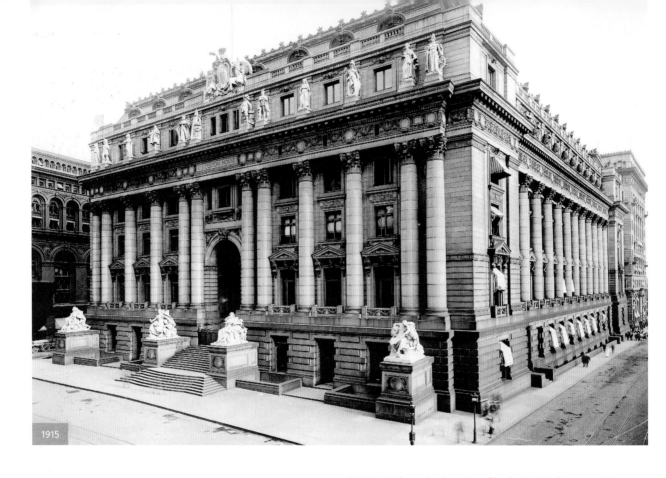

1915

U.S. CUSTOM HOUSE

The grand design reflected New York City's
premier position as the nation's center of trade

ABOVE: As the nation's center of trade, New York garnered the
lion's share of U.S. customs duties at this imposing Beaux-Arts
building, completed in 1907 in Lower Manhattan. Seen here in
1915, it was the work of Cass Gilbert, a little-known architect from
Minnesota who went on to design the Woolworth Building. Better
known at the time was the chief sculptor of the Custom House,
Daniel Chester French, who created the monumental statues at the
entrance, symbolizing the four continents of Asia, America, Europe,
and Africa.

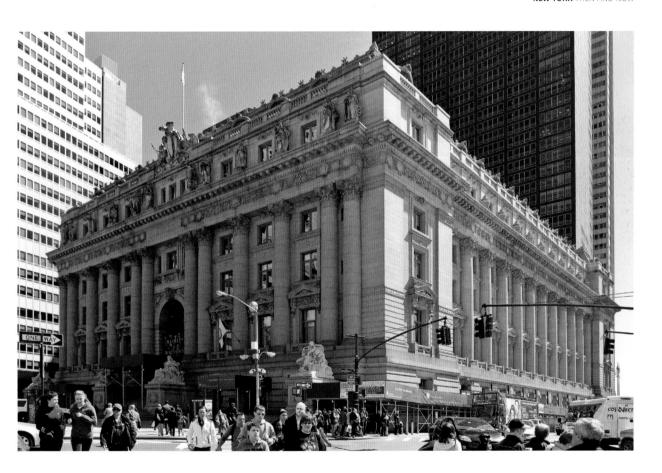

ABOVE: The original exterior belies dramatic changes inside and outside the building. After the 1950s, shipping through the Port of New York declined as the steamship companies relocated from Manhattan piers to New Jersey. Unable to maintain the lavish building, U.S. Customs moved in 1977 to modern quarters in the new World Trade Center a few blocks to the north. Empty for many years, the Custom House finally took in a new tenant, the National Museum of the American Indian, a vast collection of Indian artifacts from North, Central, and South America. Surrounded by office towers and adorned by sculpture extolling international trade, the building now celebrates Native American history before European settlement.

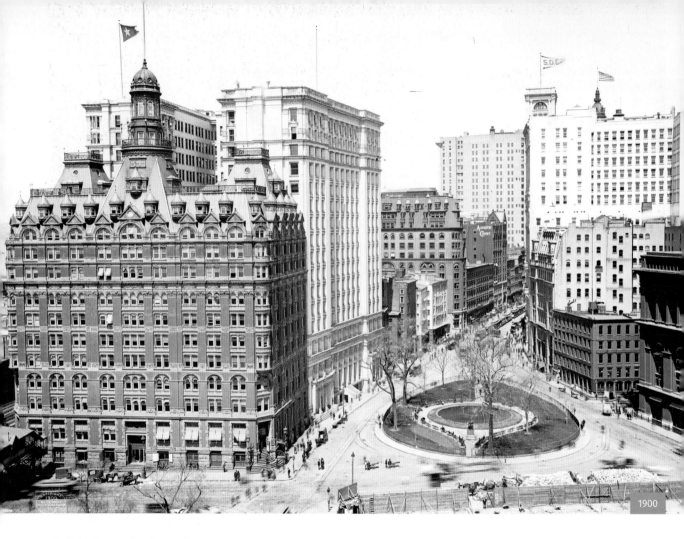

1900

BOWLING GREEN

The city's first park was the center of
colonial outrage against the British

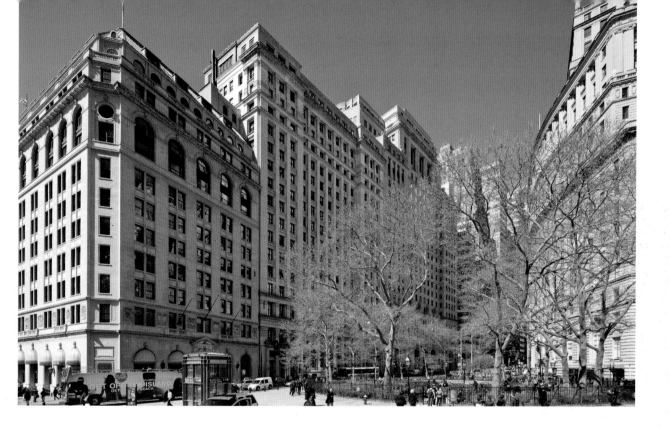

LEFT: Legend has it that the space in the center of this photo was where Peter Minuit purchased Manhattan from Native Americans in 1626. In 1733, it became New York City's first park, where lawn bowling actually took place, right at the foot of Broadway. A statue of King George III was erected in the park in 1770, surrounded a year later by an iron fence to protect it against increasingly angry colonists. In the late nineteenth century, office buildings began to rise around the park. The massive pile on the left, the Washington Building, went up in 1885, replacing a mansion. Behind it is the white Bowling Green Offices Building, built in 1898. In the right foreground is a fence for construction of the Custom House, completed several years after this 1900 photograph.

ABOVE: Taken from the steps of the Custom House, this photo shows the tiny park surrounded by other buildings that rose along with the city's fortune in the early twentieth century. The Washington Building was replaced in 1921 by One Broadway, built for the U.S. and Panama–Pacific shipping lines. On the right is the curved base of the Standard Oil Building. Its first nine stories, built in 1885, were topped by a massive tower in 1922. The Bowling Green Offices still stand on the left, but all of the other buildings from the archival photo have been replaced. The tiny park survived construction of the subway below it in the early 1900s. Rebuilt several times, it has reclaimed its eighteenth-century appearance and provides a welcome place to rest in the midst of a busy area.

NEW YORK STOCK EXCHANGE

The center of Wall Street trading actually takes place on Broad Street

BELOW: Stock traders began doing business on Wall Street as early as 1790, but the New York Stock Exchange was not formed until 1817 and the organization moved ten times before establishing its first base of operations at this site on Broad and Wall in 1865. Its grand headquarters, seen here on the left in 1919, was built in 1902. Its Roman temple facade and monumental Corinthian columns were part of the neoclassical trend sweeping the nation at the start of

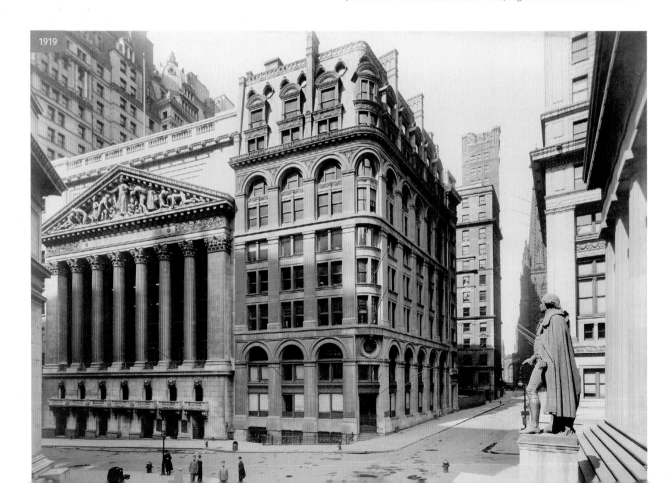

1919

the twentieth century. Next door is the Wilks Building, erected in 1890 by Matthew Wilks, who had become a wealthy man when he married into the Astor family. He acquired the site in 1882 for $330 per square foot, the highest price paid for Manhattan real estate at the time. On the far right is a statue of George Washington standing in front of Federal Hall.

BELOW: The pediment of the stock exchange contains an allegorical collection of figures representing "Integrity Protecting the Rights of Man." Over time, the figures deteriorated so badly that their stone was replaced with sheet metal. The work was done in secret, perhaps because it might have implied a state of crumbling integrity. The restored classical facade looks the same as it did in the archival photo, but behind it, the great trading floor is a technological hum of electronic activity. The Wilks Building was demolished in 1919 to make way for the exchange's twenty-three-story annex. Although the exchange is actually on Broad Street, an entrance in the annex gives it a Wall Street address. Except for a few pockmarks on the stonework of J. P. Morgan's former headquarters, the building on the far left with the red stair carpet, there are no signs of the bombing that rocked this corner in 1920. The statue of George Washington weathered the bombing without a scratch.

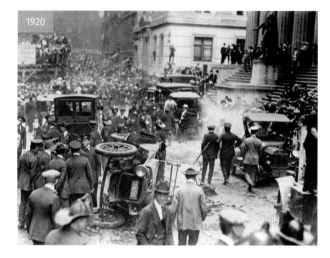

1920

ABOVE: On September 16, 1920, at the corner of Wall and Broad Street, the hub of American capitalism, a horse-drawn cart exploded into the noontime crowd. The blast killed nearly forty people, mostly clerks and stenographers on their lunch break, and wounded hundreds more. Those responsible for the violence were never discovered, although it was widely thought to be the work of anarchists. Eager to subdue fears of a stock market crash, financial leaders dispatched a battalion of sweepers and repairmen who worked through the night to remove the rubble and bloodstains from the streets. The next day, Wall Street workers, many bearing bandages, were called back to their offices, and the street returned to business as usual.

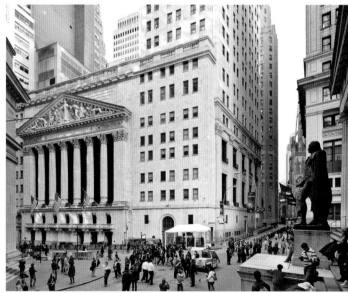

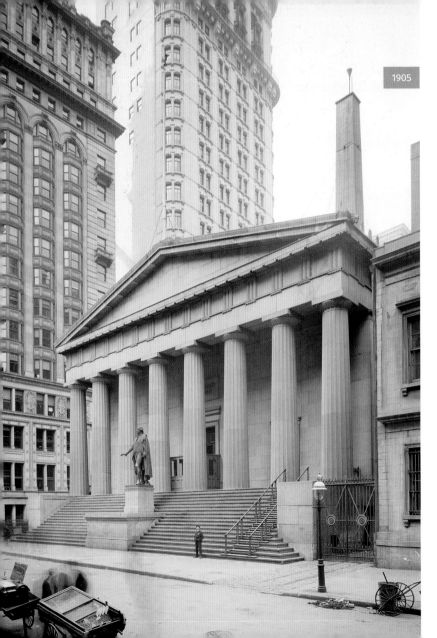

1905

FEDERAL HALL

The site of historic events
in American independence

LEFT: The statue of George Washington commemorates the spot—although not the actual building—where Washington took the oath of office as the first U.S. president in 1789. The original building was erected here at Wall and Broad Streets in 1700 as the seat of the British colonial government. John Peter Zenger was imprisoned and tried here for defending freedom of the press in 1733, and in 1765, the Stamp Act Congress met here to proclaim, "No taxation without representation." Renamed Federal Hall after the American victory, it was the place where Congress enacted the Bill of Rights in 1789. Demolished in 1812, it was replaced in 1842 by this magnificent Greek Revival building, modeled on the Parthenon. It served as the first U.S. Custom House and later as a branch of the federal treasury before becoming the National Federal Hall Memorial in 1955. The statue of Washington, by sculptor John Quincy Adams Ward, was erected here in 1883. He also had a hand in fashioning the equestrian statue of Washington in Union Square.

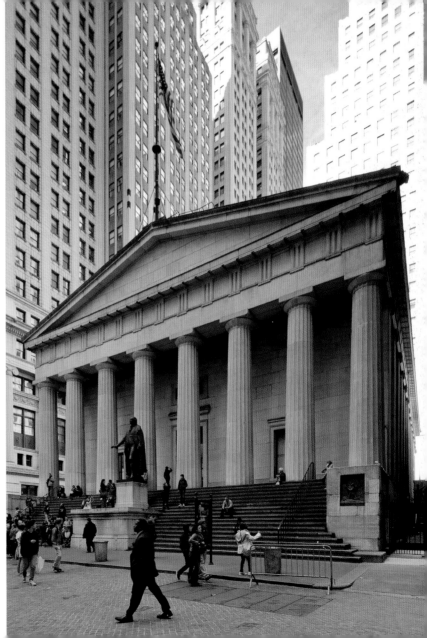

RIGHT: Although Federal Hall survived the bombing of Wall Street in 1920, the collapse of the nearby World Trade Center towers in 2001 worsened foundation cracks in the historic building. It closed in 2004 for repairs and reopened in 2006. Today the building is a museum where visitors can see the actual Bible that Washington used in his presidential inauguration, material from Zenger's famous trial, and other exhibits on the historic events that took place at this site. The beautiful rotunda (below), with its Corinthian columns, saucer dome, and ornate iron railings, is considered one of the finest Greek Revival rooms in New York City.

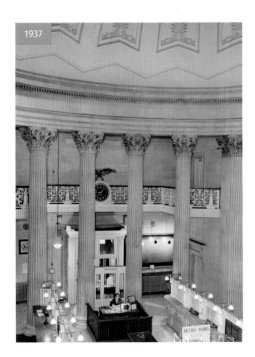

1937

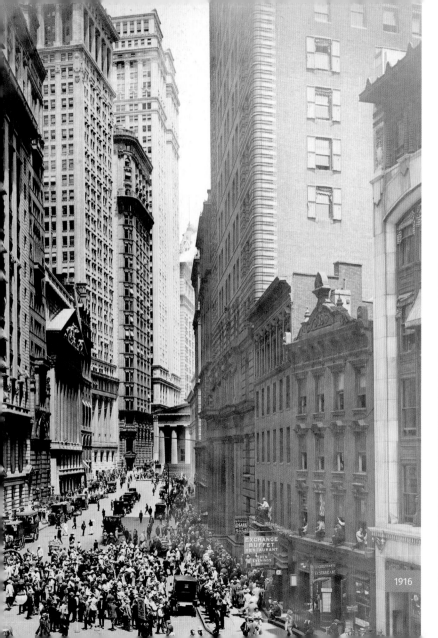

BROAD STREET

Curb brokers used hand signals to trade stocks on the street

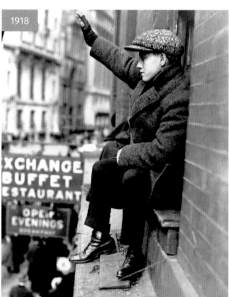

1918

1916

ABOVE: A boy on a window ledge signals to curb brokers.

OPPOSITE: The crowd of people in this 1916 photo was made up of "curb brokers," who traded stocks on the street, like bookmakers at a racetrack. Waving frenetic hand signals, they conveyed buy or sell orders to clerks in nearby buildings. The practice harks back to 1790, when brokers gathered in outdoor markets to trade government bonds covering debts incurred during the American Revolution. The New York Stock Exchange with its Greek columned facade is just up the street on the left. To its left is the Bankers Trust Company Building, the tower topped by tall, arched windows. Completed in 1912, it was considered the world's tallest structure on the smallest plot of land. J. P. Morgan had an elegant apartment on the thirty-first floor.

RIGHT: The curb exchange moved to nearby Trinity Place in 1921 and in 1953 became known as the American Stock Exchange. The same hand signals were still used inside it for decades. Broad Street began in Dutch colonial times as a wide canal extending to the East River. Lined with open markets, it was filled in as a street in 1676. A center of finance ever since the New York Stock Exchange first arrived here in 1865, the street has more recently gone through another period of change as luxury condos began to mix with historic banking offices. The building on the right, at 15 Broad Street, once part of J. P. Morgan's empire, was converted to condos in 2005. Federal Hall's Greek Revival facade can be seen at the head of the street.

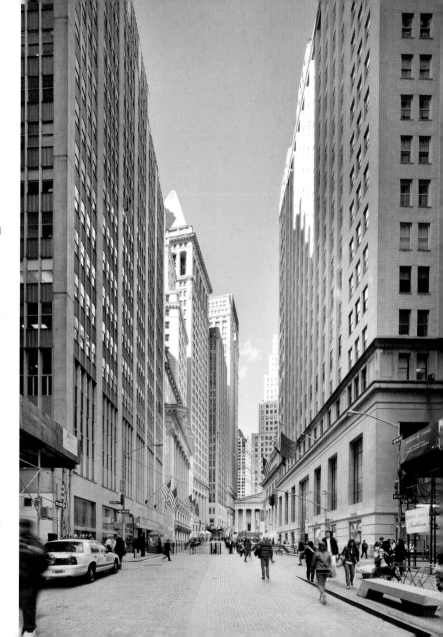

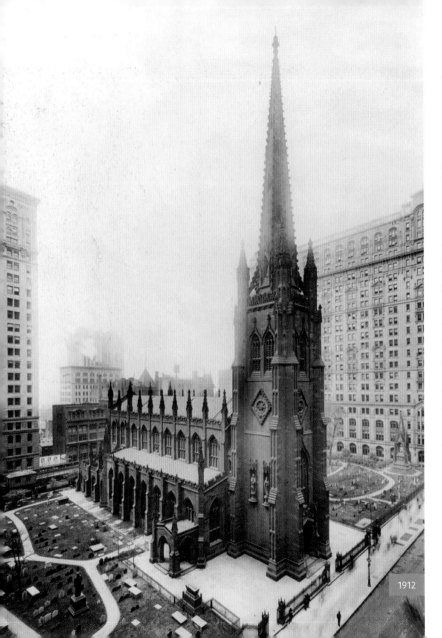

1912

TRINITY CHURCH

Pirate William "Captain" Kidd was a parishioner in the first Trinity Church

LEFT: When Richard Upjohn completed Trinity Church in 1846, its spire was the tallest structure on the city skyline and remained so for decades. But by the time of this 1912 photo, much taller buildings had already surpassed the Gothic Revival masterpiece. On the right is the white Trinity Building, erected in 1907 with Gothic detailing to harmonize with the church. As seen here, the church was actually in its third incarnation at this site on Lower Broadway. The British colonial government built the first one in 1698. The church had an unlikely parishioner in the pirate William "Captain" Kidd, who provided the block and tackle for hoisting the building stones. Kidd was a welcome figure in New York at the time, since English governors and wealthy New Yorkers often financed his lucrative raids on European ships and smuggled the loot back into the city. Both Kidd and the church came to unfortunate ends. He died on an English gallows in 1701, and the church burned in a citywide fire in 1776, likely set by American rebels at the start of the British occupation. The second version was built in 1790 but was demolished in 1839 because of structural problems.

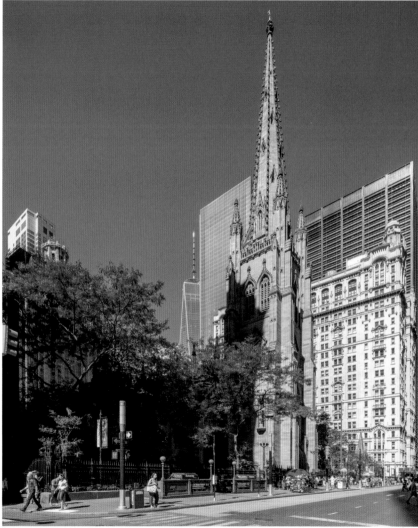

RIGHT: Trinity Church's distinctive architecture continues to stand out amid the skyscrapers that followed. On the far right is One Liberty Plaza, a steel-and-glass giant that replaced the Singer Building in the 1970s. In the far center background is One World Trade Center, whose 104 stories reach a height of 1,776 feet. In the background, immediately to the left of the church tower, is Four World Trade Center, which was completed in 2013. Standing on Lower Broadway for over 150 years, Trinity Church has also witnessed war heroes, astronauts, baseball champions, and other celebrities who have paraded through streams of ticker tape along this "Canyon of Heroes."

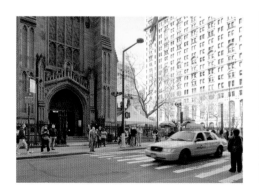

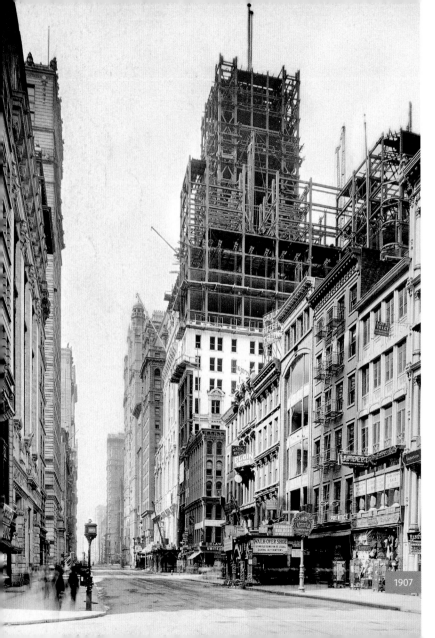

1907

SINGER BUILDING

A lost jewel of the New York skyline

LEFT: Two buildings, adjacent but very different in architectural form, are in construction in this 1907 photo. The taller one is the tower of the Singer Building. To its right is the wider City Investing Building. The Singer Sewing Machine Company had previously built a ten-story structure on this site designed by Ernest Flagg. When the company learned that City Investing was planning to build a huge structure next door, they hired Flagg to design a distinctive tower above the base of their old building. Flagg created a slender, freestanding tower that made the Singer Building forty-one stories high, the city's tallest for a short time. Even after other buildings surpassed its height, the Singer's Second Empire Baroque profile became one of New York's best known and admired landmarks.

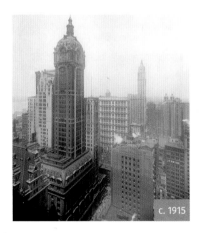

c. 1915

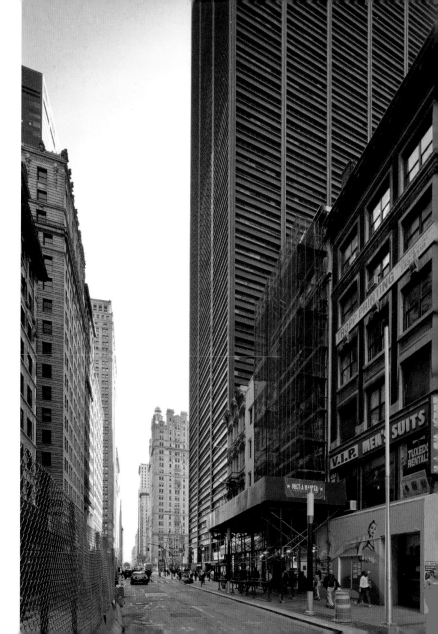

RIGHT: The hulking black monolith, the U.S. Steel Building (now One Liberty Plaza), replaced both the Singer and City Investing Buildings in 1974. The loss of the Singer Tower led to an outcry from preservationists. But no matterhow supporters praised its graceful form, the slender tower could not compete with the financial advantages of the U.S. Steel Building, which offered nearly ten times more rentable office space. The Singer Building was demolished in 1968, just as the World Trade Center towers were rising across the street. Ironically, the trade center created a glut of office space, making it hard to rent Lower Manhattan buildings for more than a decade. The Singer was the tallest building ever demolished, until the Twin Towers were destroyed in 2001.

LEFT: Looking north on Broadway from the Singer Building (foreground) to the Woolworth Building.

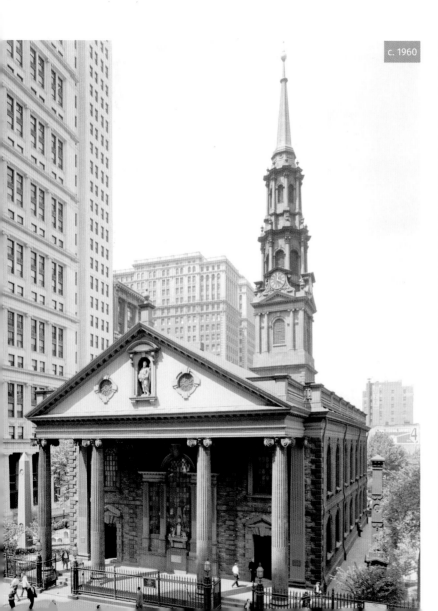

c. 1960

ST. PAUL'S CHAPEL

New York City's oldest church in continuous service

LEFT: This small chapel, a witness to the nation's most historic and tragic events, has stood its ground for nearly 250 years. Built in 1766 as a northern outpost of Trinity Church, it was just ten years old when a fire engulfed Lower Manhattan, consuming Trinity and 500 other buildings, a third of the city at the time. The chapel survived and continued to outlast even greater threats. Although commercial development swallowed nearly everything around it in the nineteenth century, the chapel continued as an active church even as skyscrapers dwarfed the tiny building throughout the twentieth century. This photo was taken before the World Trade Center towers began to rise behind St. Paul's in the 1960s. The photo below shows just how close the Twin Towers were after their completion in 1972.

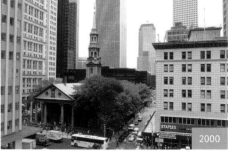

2000

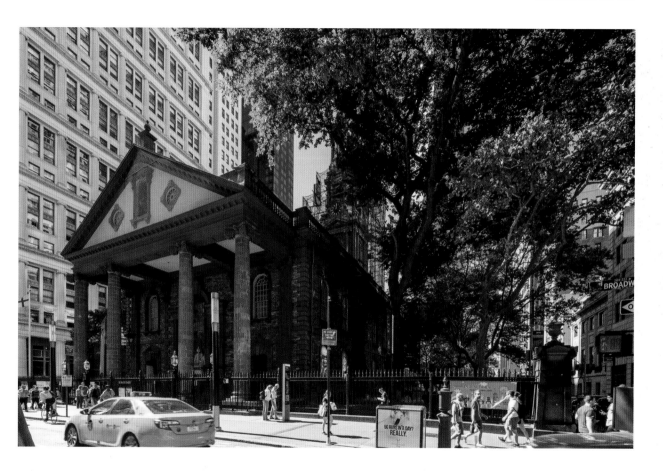

ABOVE: Built of locally quarried stone, St. Paul's is truly part of New York City's bedrock foundation and part of the land itself. Its interior columns are filled with solid oak tree trunks that grew on Manhattan's soil when it was covered with forest. Not long after the chapel was built, the land behind it, where two centuries later the Twin Towers would rise, became a rough neighborhood of taverns and brothels, ironically called "the Holy Ground." Today, the name resonates with tragic overtones for the nearly 3,000 people who perished there in 2001. Made of the stuff of history, St. Paul's has taken on new purpose and meaning as a sacred place. Behind it, hidden by trees, is One World Trade Center.

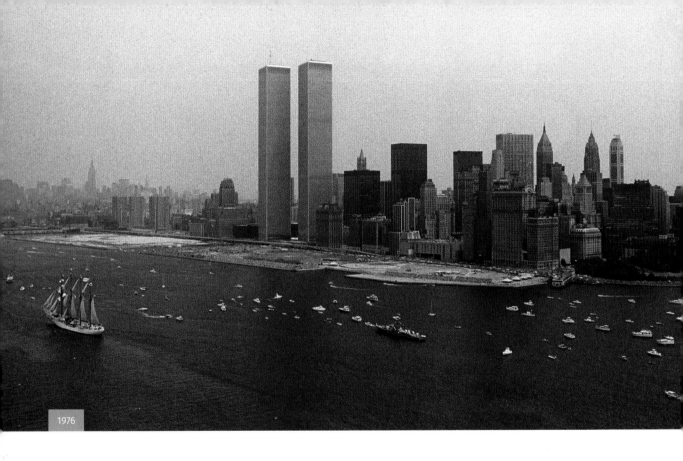

1976

WORLD TRADE CENTER

An icon of New York City reshaped by tragedy

ABOVE: The newly completed World Trade Center towers were the star of the New York waterfront on July 4, 1976, the day of this photo. The Twin Towers were part of the seven-building World Trade Center complex. Japanese architect Minoru Yamasaki began designing the complex in 1962, and the first buildings opened in 1970. The Twin Towers, each 110 stories tall, opened in 1976, becoming the tallest buildings in the world and redefining the Manhattan skyline. The excavation for the Twin Towers created an enormous volume of landfill, adding ninety-two acres to Manhattan, shown here as the flat expanse along the shoreline.

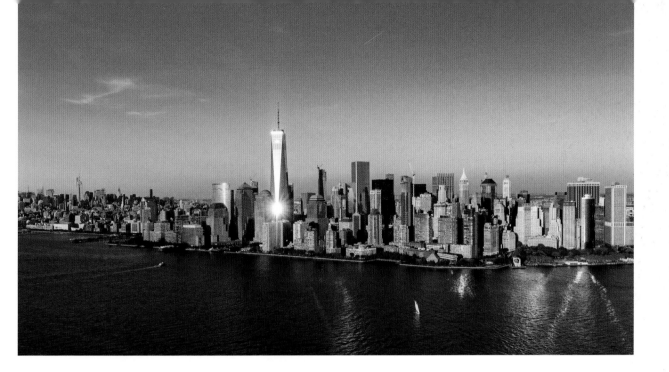

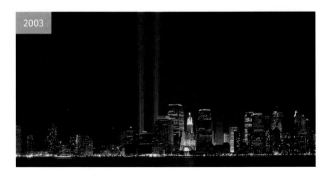

2003

ABOVE: Beginning in 2002, a group of architects and artists placed eighty-eight searchlights on the trade center site simulating the Twin Towers in an annual "Tribute of Light."

ABOVE: The 104-story One World Trade Center, the first building to rise at Ground Zero, was completed in 2014. It reaches 1,776 feet, a symbol of the year of American independence and more than 400 feet higher than the Twin Towers. Its unusual shape is made up of eight elongated triangles above a twenty-story square base. A unique memorial fountain, covering the two footprints of the original Twin Towers, was dedicated in 2011. Below the surface, the vast infrastructure destroyed along with the Twin Towers has been restored. Trains are running underground again between the World Trade Center Station and New Jersey. New retaining walls and electrical, plumbing, and communication cables were also laid for construction of four additional towers. The new swath of land created by the original excavation became Battery Park City and the World Financial Center, a residential and office complex of astounding size and distinguished architectural design built in the 1980s.

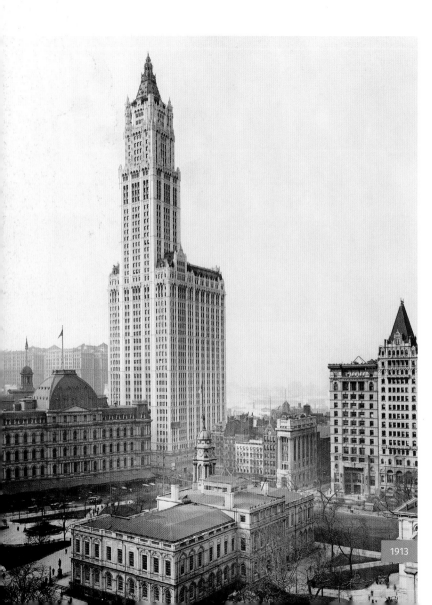

WOOLWORTH BUILDING
Frank Woolworth's investment paid off

LEFT: Just beginning its seventeen-year reign as the world's tallest structure, the newly completed Woolworth Building towers above Broadway and City Hall Park in this 1913 view. It was created by F. W. Woolworth, the founder of the five-and-dime-store chain, and Cass Gilbert, architect of the U.S. Custom House. Called the "Cathedral of Commerce," it has Gothic pointed arches, making the building soar to a pinnacled crown. Taken from the northeast, the photo includes the domed post office building that once dominated City Hall Park. Critics called the massive post office "a boil on the end of a man's nose" because it blocked views of the park and City Hall. It was demolished in the 1930s. The photo below shows the tower nearing completion.

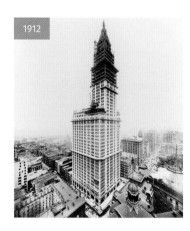

1912

1913

RIGHT: Like all great skyscrapers, the Woolworth Building's height, sixty stories, was not the only reason for its lasting fame. It lost its title as the world's tallest to the Chrysler Building in 1930 and was dwarfed by the World Trade Center towers in the 1970s. Although the Twin Towers were just a few blocks away, their fall caused only minor damage to the Woolworth Building. The new World Trade Center tower and a number of other skyscrapers built since 2001 now stand behind the Woolworth Building. Modernist architects in the 1950s disdained the Woolworth's ornate neo-Gothic facade, but after decades of spare, modern buildings, it has proven them wrong. The building's architecture now gets the praise it deserves, and Frank Woolworth's investment has also paid off. He built the structure for about $13 million, and after retaining ownership for eighty-five years, his company sold it in 1998 for $155 million. The spiky white building on the left is the new World Trade Center Transportation Hub, designed by Spanish architect Santiago Calatrava.

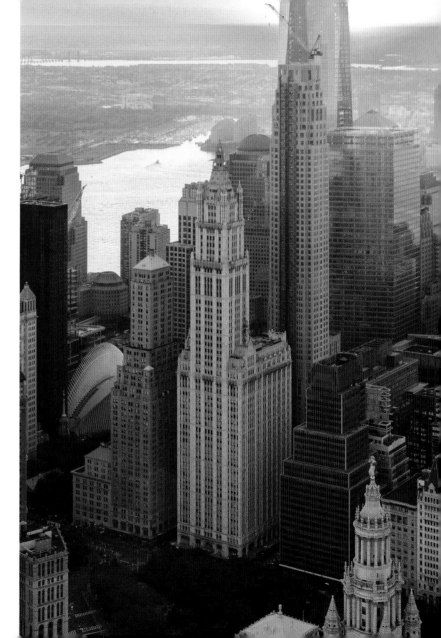

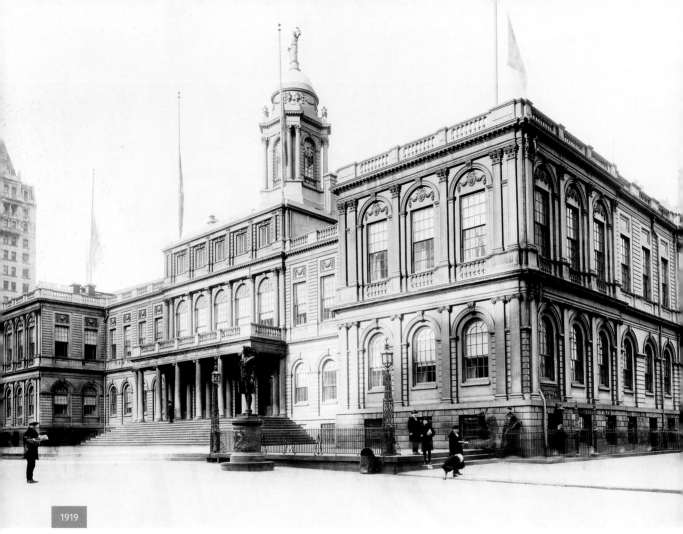

1919

CITY HALL

A rare fixture in a city known for constant change

LEFT: In this 1919 view, City Hall looked much as it did when it was completed in 1811—no small feat since there had been efforts to demolish and redesign it in the nineteenth century. In one of the city's earliest historic preservation campaigns, a group of New Yorkers convinced officials that demolishing City Hall would be an "act of vandalism." Although the building survived, its condition deteriorated for many years.

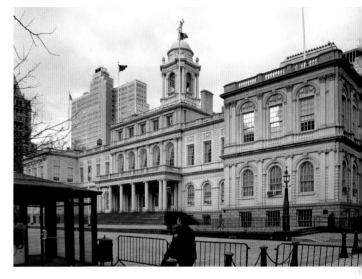

BELOW: In this 1893 view, City Hall (left) is just steps away from the towering buildings of Newspaper Row, where nearly twenty daily papers kept a close eye on the government. The domed tower, completed in 1890, was the headquarters of the *New York World*, whose hard-driving publisher Joseph Pulitzer tracked down every scent of scandal. The pyramidal tower on the far right topped the offices of the *New York Tribune*, founded by the legendary editor Horace Greeley, who died in 1872, three years before his new building was completed.

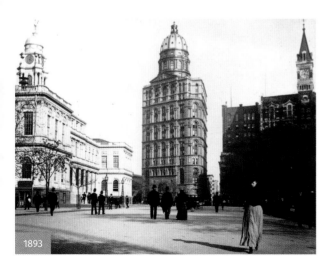

1893

ABOVE: Shortly after the 1919 photo was taken, a fire nearly destroyed the copper cupola. Its original marble exterior eroded and the rear of the building, covered in cheaper brownstone, remained unfinished for decades. City Hall's marble exterior was finally replaced by limestone in the 1950s, and this time, the white facade also covered the building's brownstone back. The historic interior has been beautifully restored in more recent years. The small, elegant building is still the center of government, where New York City's mayor and city council conduct daily business as they have for nearly two centuries. However, security threats after September 11 have made the building off-limits to the public. Fenced and heavily guarded, it is open only to those on official business.

TWEED COURTHOUSE

An architectural treasure with a scandalous namesake

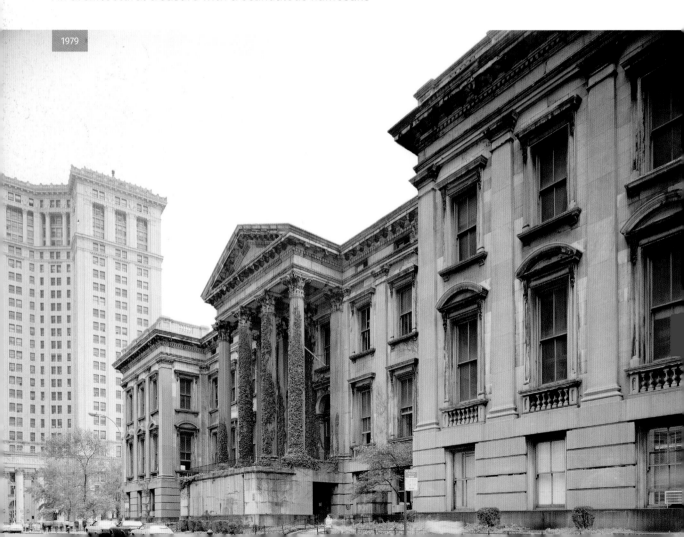

1979

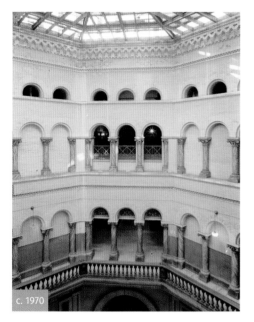

c. 1970

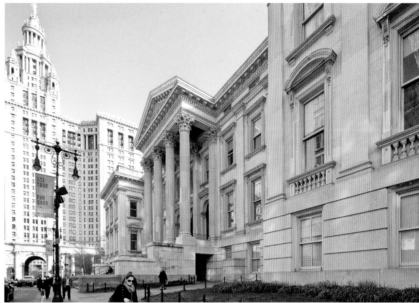

LEFT: The courthouse is informally named for William "Boss" Tweed, the corrupt politician who controlled New York City from the 1860s to the early 1870s. A rotund figure who wore a large diamond in his shirtfront, Tweed was the king of kickbacks. He extracted millions of dollars from contractors by grossly inflating the costs of public projects. He and his cronies made off with a sizable chunk of the twelve million dollars spent on building the courthouse. Construction began in 1861, but by the time the building's shell was finally completed in 1872, the scheme had been exposed in the newspapers. A year later, Tweed was tried and convicted in an unfinished courtroom.

ABOVE: The multistory, domed rotunda, added in 1881, is a magnificent feature of the courthouse. It was designed by Leopold Eidlitz, who also worked on the New York State Capitol in Albany.

ABOVE: Handsomely restored with a grand staircase in 2003, the former courthouse has regained its dignity and taken on a new purpose. Its interior rooms, grown shabby over the years as city offices, were restored to their historic splendor as the new home of the city's Department of Education. The restoration, begun in 1999, removed eighteen layers of interior paint in order to reveal the original colors. In an ironic tribute to Tweed, the building known by his name and tainted by his corruption is now recognized as one of the city's greatest achievements of civic architecture. On the left, the Municipal Building, completed in 1914, is visible here as it was in the earlier photo.

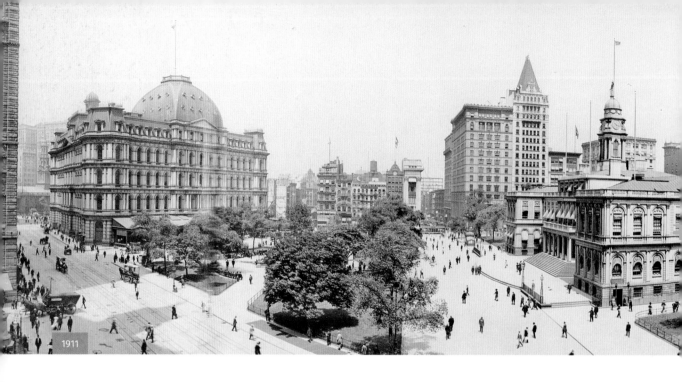

1911

PARK ROW AND CITY HALL PARK

Transportation reshaped the city

ABOVE: The horizontal structure in this 1911 view is the Manhattan Terminal of the Brooklyn Bridge, an elevated station for the trolley cars and trains that crossed the bridge. Trolleys replaced the original cable car system in 1898, and by 1907, sixty electric trains an hour were running across the bridge. The terminal was enlarged several times, projecting beyond Park Row into City Hall Park. Directly behind City Hall is the Tweed Courthouse with its domed rotunda.

RIGHT: Trains eventually gave way to cars, and the old terminal was dismantled in 1944. In this elevated view of City Hall, the building is once again undergoing restoration to maintain the 200-year-old structure. The Municipal Building (right of center) now houses 2,000 employees. On the far right, the boxy, redbrick building is One Police Plaza, headquarters of the New York City Police Department, the largest force in the country.

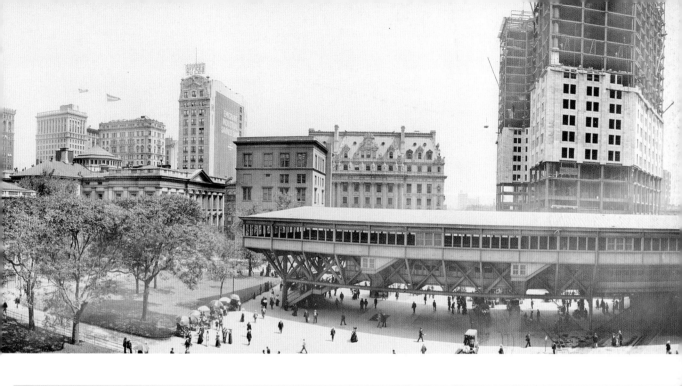
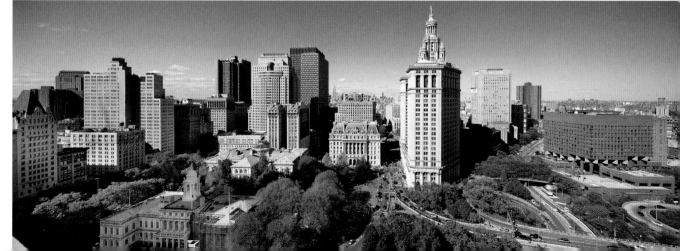

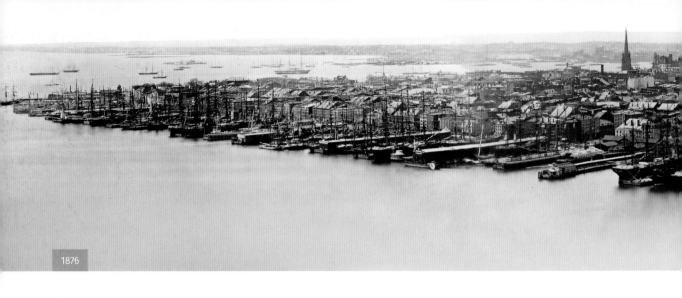

1876

ABOVE: The Manhattan tower of the bridge was built in 1876, the year this picture was taken and seven years before the span and cables were finally strung across the river. The photo was taken from the top of the tower on the Brooklyn side, which went up first. The Manhattan tower proved more difficult to build, as workers had to dig down nearly eighty feet under the river before reaching a stable foundation, almost twice the depth as for the Brooklyn tower. This difficult and dangerous work was done in huge, airtight caissons. Rising more than 276 feet above the water, the Manhattan tower dominates the city skyline. The large, domed building in the background, just left of the bridge tower, is the old post office (1875) in City Hall Park.

RIGHT: Seen from a helicopter hovering over the bridge, Manhattan is now a completely different city. The tallest building on the skyline is the uniquely shaped One World Trade Center. Nearby, on the right is the 8 Spruce Street tower designed by Frank Gehry—one of the tallest residential buildings in the city. The East River waterfront is no longer an active port, but a few tall-masted ships still dock at the South Street Seaport. The large pier near the bridge is the Seaport's Pier 17 Pavilion.

MANHATTAN FROM THE BROOKLYN BRIDGE

The bridge tower was once Manhattan's tallest structure

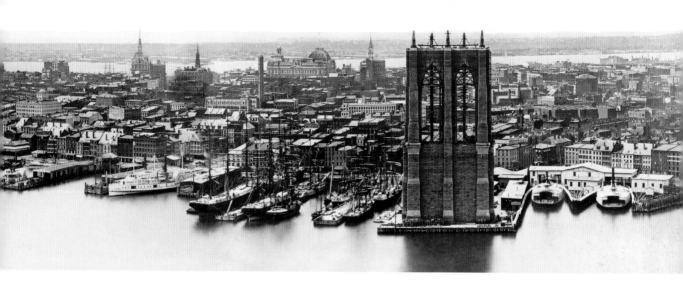
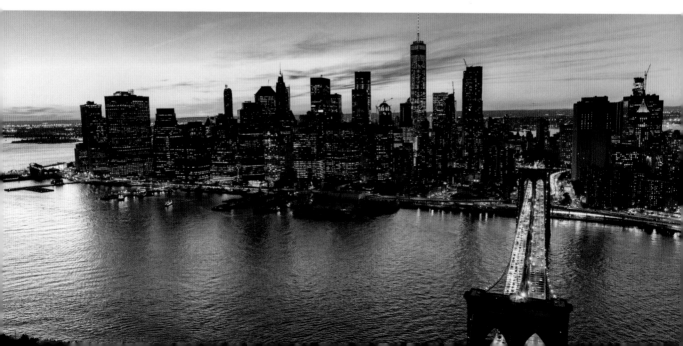

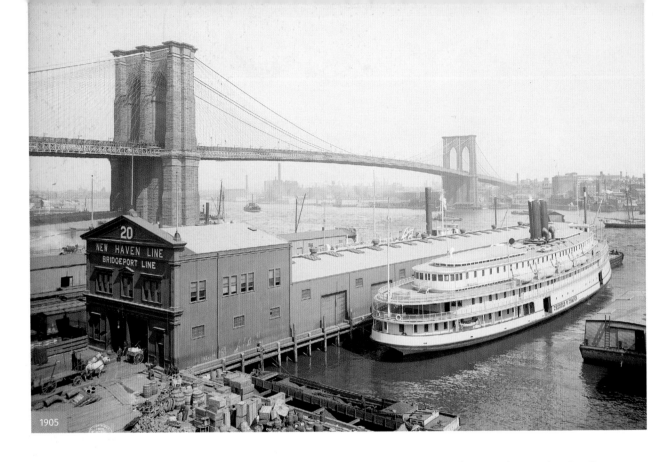

1905

BROOKLYN BRIDGE

A wonder of the nineteenth century and a
timeless structure of the modern city

ABOVE: This photo was taken more than two decades after
the bridge opened in 1883, the first to span the East River.
Proposed in 1857 by German-born engineer John Augustus
Roebling, construction of the bridge finally got underway in 1869.
Roebling was killed in an accident shortly afterward, and his son,
Washington Roebling, took over the work. Injured in one of the
caissons, the younger Roebling became an invalid, but with his
wife's help, he supervised the project from his bedside window
across the river in Brooklyn. It took fourteen years and $16 million
to complete, three times the estimated cost.

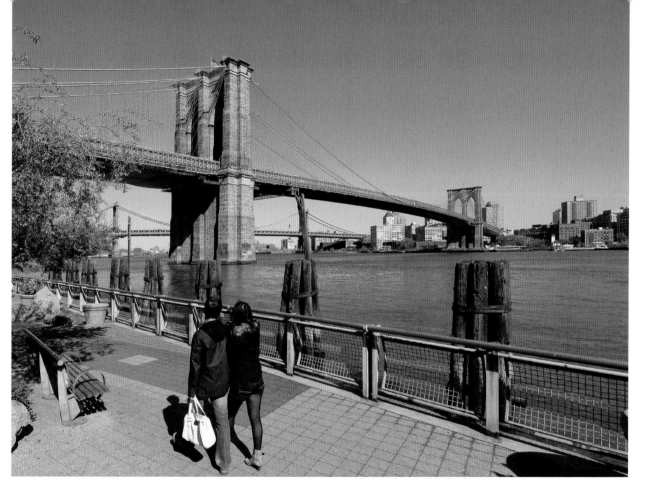

ABOVE: As cars and trucks supplanted ships and boats, the Brooklyn Bridge proved to be a lasting structure in the modern world with relatively few changes. Nineteenth-century New Yorkers, crossing on cable cars, horse-drawn trolleys, and electric trains, could not have imagined how the bridge would prove adaptable to motorized vehicles. The bridge was built so well that for the first seventy years of its life, well into the age of the automobile, it required only routine maintenance. In 1953, the deck was strengthened to bear the weight of increased motor traffic. No longer the largest or most innovative, the bridge still captures the imagination for its grace and beauty. The benches and walkway along the newly completed East River Esplanade provide a perfect place to enjoy the view. The Manhattan Bridge, a later span between Manhattan and Brooklyn, is on the left.

BROOKLYN BRIDGE WALKWAY

Crossing the bridge on foot is one of the city's great experiences

BELOW: From the day it opened, the Brooklyn Bridge attracted a steady flow of pedestrians. But a tragic accident occurred on Memorial Day 1883, just a week after the opening. In the crush of an uncontrollably large crowd on the stairway leading to the bridge, panic broke out and twelve people were trampled to death. The number of police officers on the bridge was increased. A year after the accident, impresario P. T. Barnum marched a herd of twenty-one elephants over the bridge to demonstrate its strength.

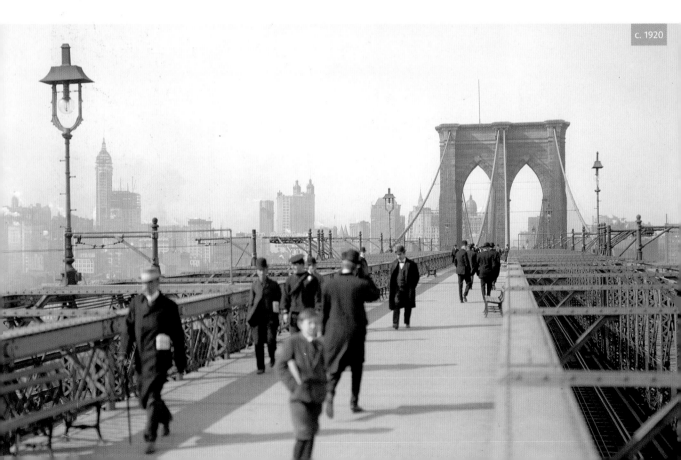

c. 1920

BELOW: A new generation of walkers, runners, and bike riders have made the bridge so popular that lines were painted down the walkway to keep them from bumping into each other. Many Brooklynites walk to work and back home over the bridge. At lunchtime, it becomes a running track for office workers. Despite the noise from cars driving on the roadway twelve feet below, crossing the bridge on foot or bicycle is one of the city's great experiences. The stone arches and powerful cables spun from steel, a material still new in the mid-nineteenth century, remain constants in the city's ever-changing skyline.

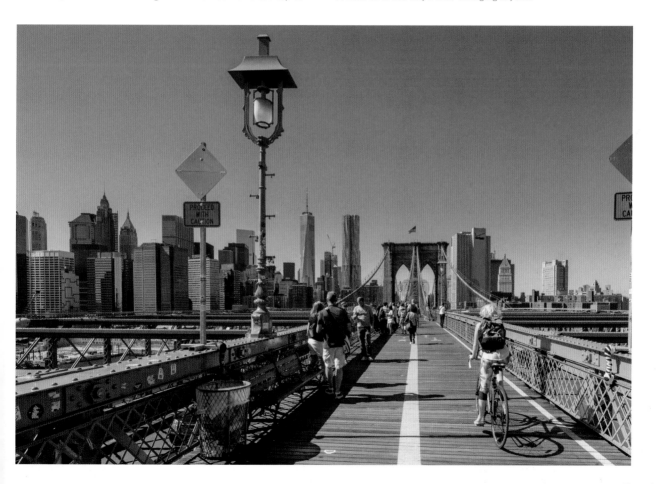

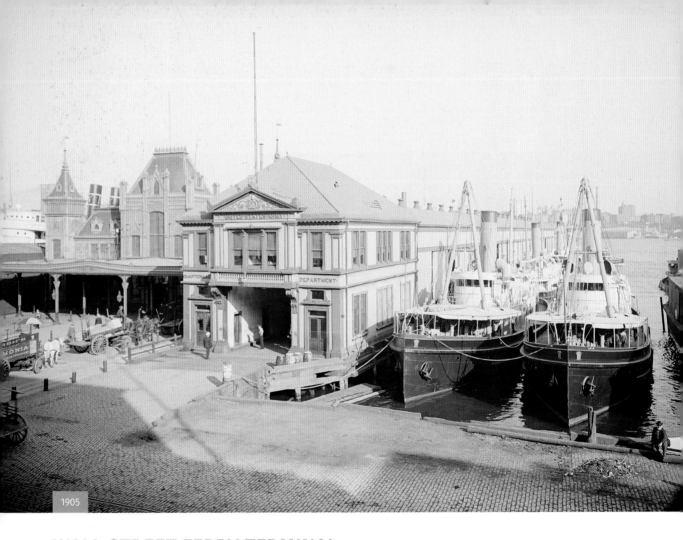

1905

WALL STREET FERRY TERMINAL

A resurgence in ferry service is reconnecting
New York to its waterfront history

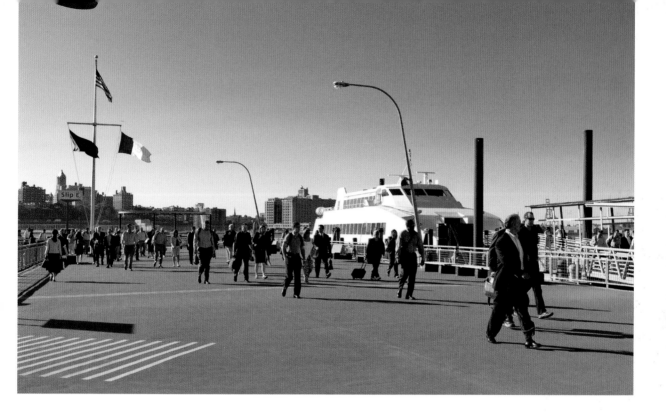

LEFT: As a city of islands, New York's lifeline was its arterial network of ferries. Before and even after the bridges were built, dozens of ferry lines plied the waters connecting Manhattan, the other New York boroughs, and New Jersey. This 1905 photo shows the ferry terminal on the East River at the foot of Wall Street and the adjacent government dock with two ships from the Army Quartermaster Corps, then based at Governors Island. The ferries were essential to commuters and commercial operations, as seen by the horse and carts lined up to board. From its earliest days, East River commerce in this area created the financial heart of Wall Street. The many goods arriving in New York were registered at Wall Street futures exchanges, the predecessors of the New York Stock Exchange.

ABOVE: By the mid-twentieth century, bridges, tunnels, and the onslaught of automobiles had replaced nearly every ferry service to Manhattan—except the one to Staten Island. Elevated highways ringing Manhattan's shoreline also cut off access to the waterfront. But the new Wall Street Ferry Terminal managed to break through the barriers and reconnect people to waterborne transportation. With cars clogging the bridges and tunnels and polluting the air, federal funds became available as an incentive for the rebirth of ferry service. Jutting out from the East River, the sleek pier built at Wall and South Streets in 2000 provides dock space for several private lines connecting Manhattan, New Jersey, Brooklyn, and Queens.

MANHATTAN BRIDGE ENTRANCE

A survivor of the ravages of time

BELOW: In the early twentieth century, a generation after the wonder of the Brooklyn Bridge, suspension bridges over the East River were becoming a common sight. This is the grand entrance to the Manhattan Bridge, completed in 1909 as the third suspension bridge to span the river between Manhattan and Brooklyn. Its steel towers can be seen in the right background. The entrance, seen here in its final days of construction, was not completed until 1912. Called the Court of Honor, it was designed by Carrère and Hastings, the architects who were just finishing the New York Public Library. Both structures are impressive monuments of classical design.

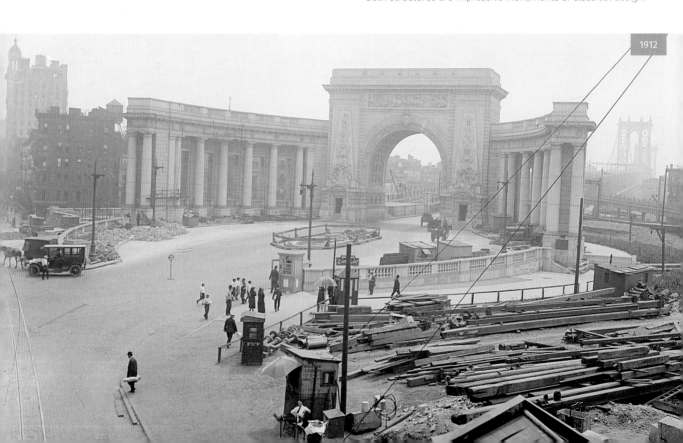

1912

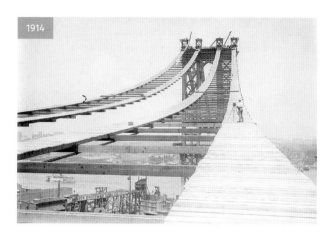

1914

LEFT: A photographer takes up a perilous position on the temporary footpath set up during construction of the Manhattan Bridge.

BELOW: The bridge was soon overwhelmed by traffic. Located on the Bowery at Canal Street on the Lower East Side, it became a portal in the early twentieth century for immigrants moving from tenements to slightly better quarters in Brooklyn. By the 1970s, some traffic engineers saw this majestic colonnade as just another deteriorating part of the bridge and wanted to remove it. However, cracks discovered in the structure of the bridge itself, which carried subway trains as well as cars, were the major concern. Three decades and $646 million later, the bridge and the colonnade are in much better shape. It is now the Manhattan entrance to Chinatown, and on the Brooklyn side, to the trendy enclave known as DUMBO (Down Under the Manhattan Bridge Overpass).

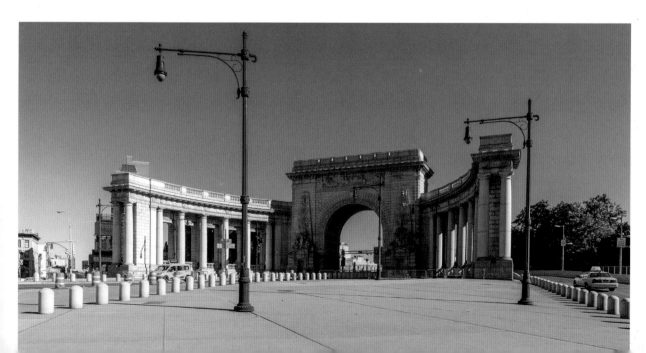

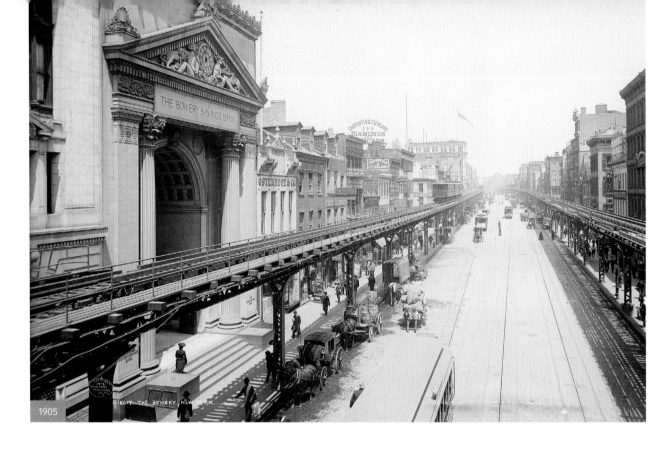

1905

BOWERY SAVINGS BANK

The grand building outlived the bank

ABOVE: Rising above its surroundings, this splendid building was completed in 1895, a few blocks north of the Manhattan Bridge. Neither the elevated train tracks on the Bowery, erected in 1878, nor the surrounding working-class neighborhood were seen as obstacles to the concept. The architect for the building, Stanford White, created a classical design fit for a Roman emperor. Corinthian columns and a grand arched entrance led to an awe-inspiring interior. The financial panic of 1893 had rocked the economy, but these impressive chambers inspired confidence. In 1905 the Bowery Bank claimed to be the "largest and most successful savings bank in the world."

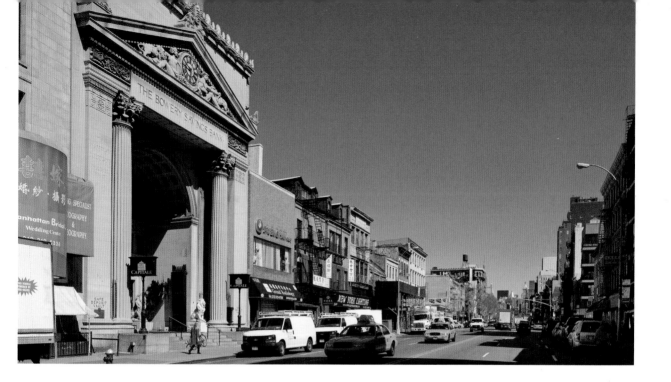

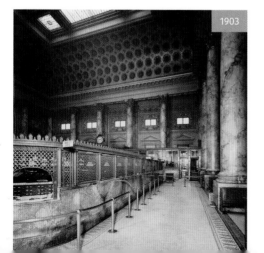

1903

ABOVE: In the 1920s, the Bowery Savings Bank moved its headquarters uptown to East Forty-second Street, but kept a branch in this building until 1982, outlasting the elevated tracks, which came down in the 1950s. However, the bank began to suffer losses in the 1970s. Sold several times over the years, the building was ultimately converted in 2002 to a restaurant and catering hall. Now called Capitale, it draws plenty of new money from an upscale crowd for special events. Much of the surrounding Lower East Side neighborhood is a hip location today, and the bank's impressive interior serves as a grand ballroom for weddings, New Year's Eve parties, and fashion-show galas. The name of the banking entity disappeared in a corporate shuffle, but is still ensconced on its magnificent building.

LEFT: The bank's interior was a magnificent display of marble—on the walls, mosaic floors, columns, and teller counters—all gorgeously lit by the amber-domed skylight set in a gilded coffered ceiling. The interior is now a glamorous setting for special events.

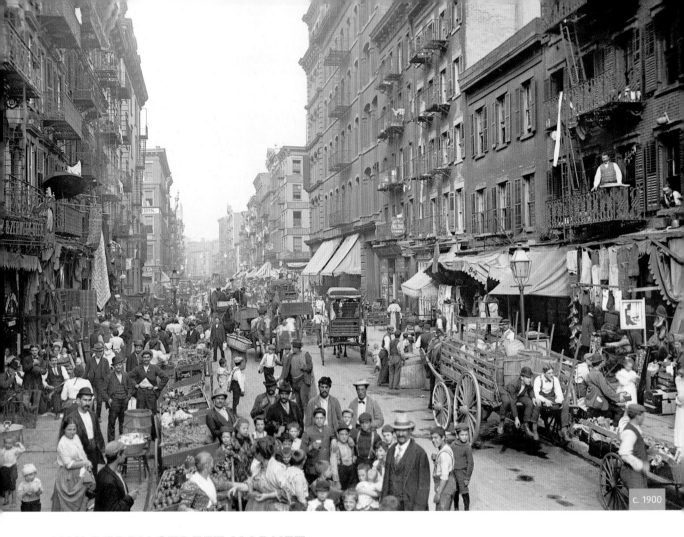

c. 1900

MULBERRY STREET MARKET

Outdoor markets relieved desperately
overcrowded tenements

LEFT: Mulberry Street was the heart of Little Italy, the Italian American enclave that rapidly expanded on Manhattan's Lower East Side in the wake of huge waves of immigration from 1899 to 1910. Fewer than 20,000 Italians lived in the city in 1880. By 1910, there were over half a million, more than in any other American city. Like other immigrant groups, they lived in desperately overcrowded tenements, relieved somewhat by daily outdoor markets where they shared the language, food, and customs of their homeland. "When the sun shines, the entire population seeks the street," Jacob Riis wrote in his 1890 book, *How the Other Half Lives*. The vibrant, at times violent, atmosphere of this densely packed area was brought to life in the film *Godfather II* in a murder scene that takes place during a parade on Mulberry Street. The photo below shows a clam seller on Mulberry Street.

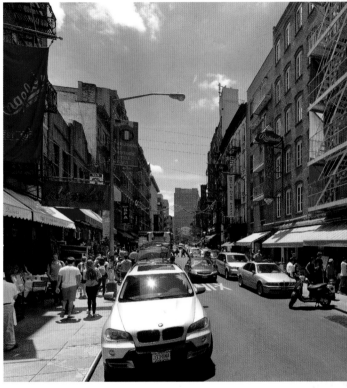

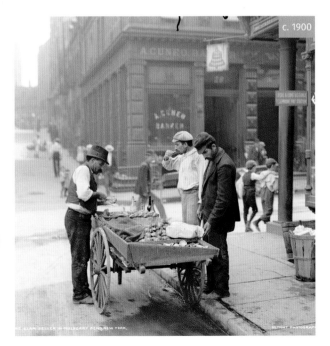

c. 1900

ABOVE: Historically, Little Italy extended for dozens of blocks all around Mulberry Street. Over the years, as Italians moved to other areas and Chinese immigrants moved in, the Italian section shrank to just a few blocks on Mulberry Street alone. Lined with Italian restaurants and shops, it draws locals and tourists seeking the flavors of the old neighborhood. This condensed core of Italian culture temporarily expands every September for the Feast of San Gennaro, an outdoor festival all along Mulberry Street. For the rest of the year, most of the area returns to Chinatown.

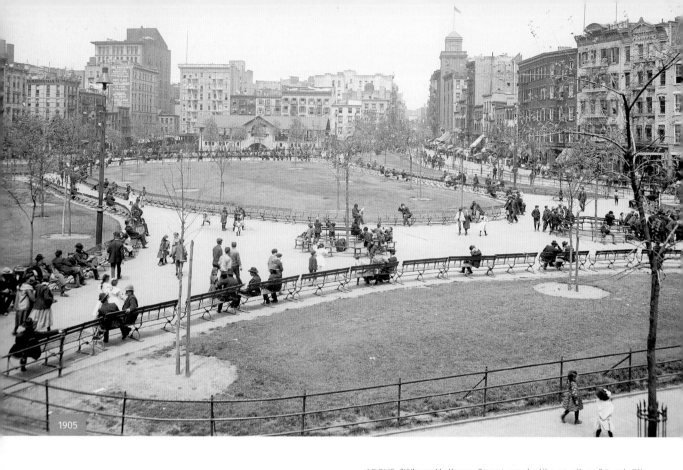

1905

MULBERRY BEND

The park was built to eradicate the deadliest part of the neighborhood

ABOVE: "Where Mulberry Street crooks like an elbow," Jacob Riis wrote in 1890, "is the foul core of New York's slums." As a police photographer, Riis knew this maze of tenements and back alleys all too well. He railed against it for years, recording the filthy conditions and high crime and infant mortality rates. The park at Mulberry Bend was created to eradicate this blight, the deadliest part of the notorious Five Points neighborhood. Located at the intersection of five streets, it created a triangular plot of land ironically known as Paradise Park. It was designed in 1897 by Calvert Vaux, one of the designers of Central Park.

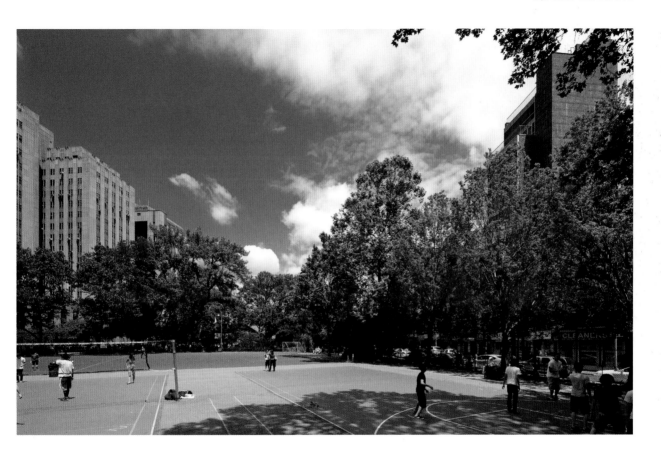

ABOVE: The violence of the Five Points neighborhood was graphically portrayed in the 2002 film *The Gangs of New York*. A reminder of this infamous history remains in the Criminal Court buildings adjacent to the park on the left. But the park shows no evidence of the notorious sites that once blighted the area, places that Jacob Riis described in *How the Other Half Lives* as Bandits' Roost, Murderers' Alley, and Ragpickers' Row. Mulberry Bend was renamed Columbus Park in 1911 in honor of the Italian explorer Christopher Columbus, a reflection of its surrounding Italian population. In later years, it was engulfed by a growing Chinatown. The pavilion in the background of the archival photo was rebuilt over the years, but is still there. Basketball courts and new playground equipment have been added, attracting people of different ages and cultures.

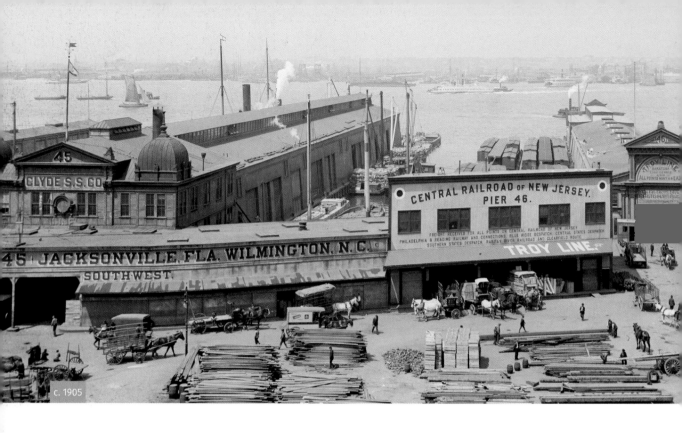

c. 1905

ABOVE: The large ship on the right, the RMS *Baltic*, was part of the White Star Line, the British shipping company that built the *Titanic*. If that ill-fated ship had not sunk in 1912, it would have docked several blocks north of this site near West Sixteenth Street. These piers, located near West Tenth Street, served many kinds of vessels, like those loading railroad cars and building materials at Piers 45 and 46. The *Baltic*, launched in 1903 as the largest ship in the world, carried nearly 3,000 passengers between Liverpool and New York, 2,000 of whom traveled in steerage. In World War I, the *Baltic* carried the first U.S. troops to Europe in May 1917.

HUDSON RIVER PIERS

A sister ship of the *Titanic* docked here

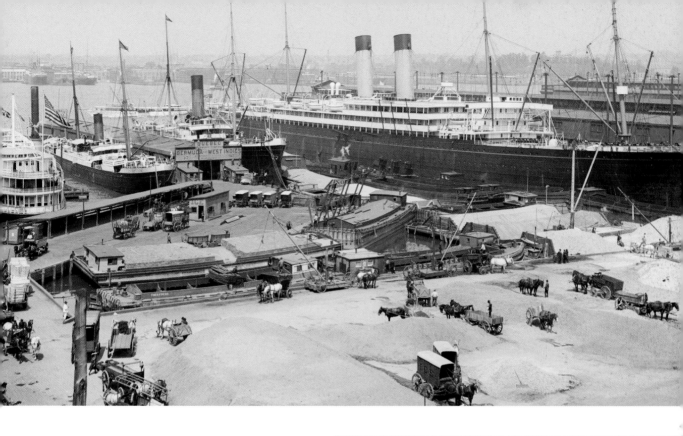

RIGHT: In 1934, White Star merged with its chief rival, Cunard Lines, which adopted the term "White Star service" to attract first-class passengers. But the age of great liners docking in New York ended in the second half of the twentieth century when shipping companies moved from Manhattan's crowded piers to new and larger ports across the Hudson River in New Jersey. All along Manhattan's waterfront, the piers became a postindustrial wasteland. In the 1990s, the Hudson River waterfront was transformed into a five-mile-long park. This section was the first to sprout trees, flower beds, and new recreation piers built over the remains of the old docks. The yellow water taxi is a small reminder of the area's shipping history.

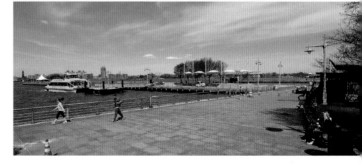

THE HIGH LINE

An elevated railway became a park in the sky

BELOW: Elevated thirty feet above the ground, this rail freight line ran for a mile and a half through Manhattan's Lower West Side, snaking around, between, and sometimes right through buildings to deliver goods to factories and warehouses. It was built in the 1930s as part of an improvement project to get the freight trains off the streets, where they were congesting traffic and causing deadly accidents. But accidents kept happening. One of the main routes, Tenth Avenue, was known as "Death Avenue." When the trains began to run on the High Line, it was hailed as a transformation of the West Side.

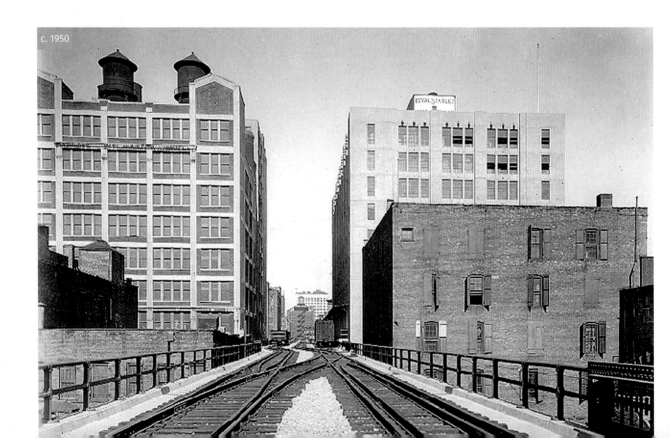

c. 1950

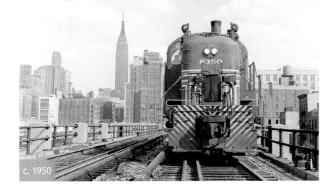

c. 1950

ABOVE: The steel viaduct was built strong enough to hold two freight trains on separate tracks. This section looking toward the Empire State Building is an east–west spur off the north–south main line.

BELOW: Now a park in the sky, the High Line has brought about an extraordinary transformation of the Lower West Side, although one completely unexpected in its days as a railway. From its start, the freight operation was a disappointment. The Great Depression cut the number of shipments in half, and after World War II, trucks reduced train freight to a trickle. The last train on the elevated track delivered its last load, a shipment of frozen turkeys, in 1980. The abandoned line became a blight, but a group of community residents saw it as an opportunity. After decades of debate, the Friends of the High Line succeeded in stopping its demolition and raised funds to turn it into a park. It opened in 2009, enhanced with landscaping amid the old tracks. Immediately popular, the aerial greenway gives New Yorkers a new perspective, above and through the city.

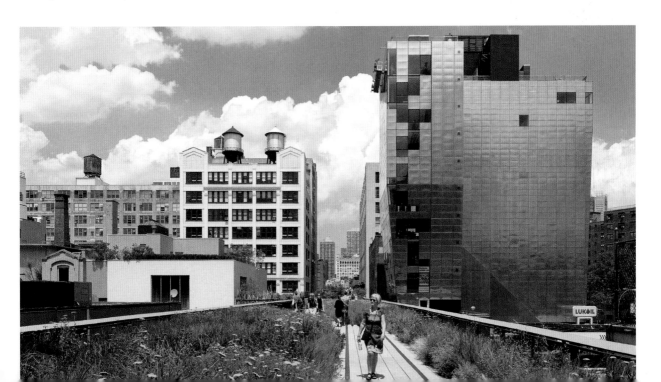

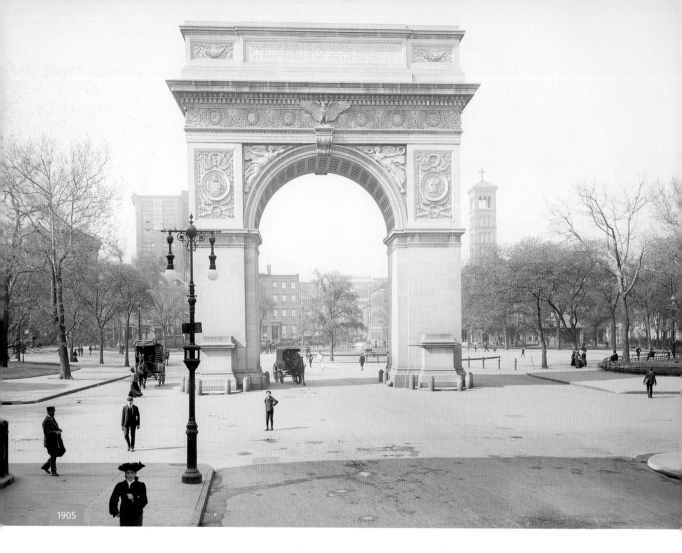

1905

WASHINGTON SQUARE ARCH

The quintessential landmark of Greenwich Village

1918

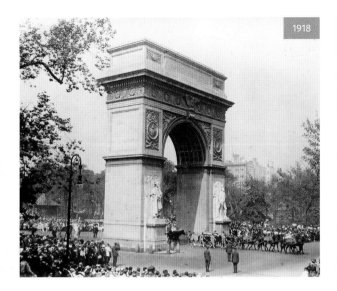

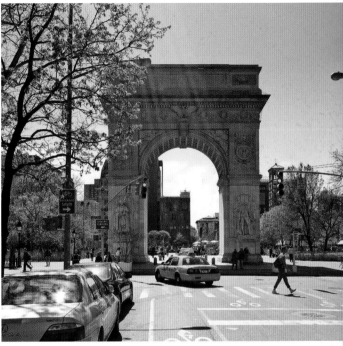

LEFT: The striking marble arch at the head of Fifth Avenue in Washington Square Park is just ten years old in this 1905 photo. It was preceded by a wood-and-plaster version commemorating the centennial of George Washington's inauguration as president in 1789. The temporary arch proved so popular that a committee of local residents from this fashionable neighborhood raised $80,000 to build the permanent arch and hired Stanford White, then at the height of his career, to design it. In this view looking south toward the park, two pedestals at either side of the base of the arch stand empty, awaiting the placement of two statues of George Washington. In the right background is the tower of Judson Memorial Church, also designed by White, and completed a year after the arch in 1896.

ABOVE: Passing under the arch in 1918 is the funeral procession of Mayor John Purroy Mitchel, known as the "boy mayor," who died at the age of thirty-nine in a plane crash in the last days of World War I.

ABOVE: In 1906, just a year after the archival photo, Stanford White was shot and killed by the husband of his former mistress. In 1917, the arch became a symbol of bohemian Greenwich Village when artists John Sloan and Marcel Duchamp and a group of their friends climbed to the top and proclaimed that the Village had seceded from the Union and would thenceforth be the "Free and Independent Republic of Washington Square." The two statues of Washington, sculpted by Herman MacNeil and Alexander Stirling Calder, were not placed at the arch until 1918. Today the arch is Greenwich Village's most recognizable landmark, so closely associated with the neighborhood that few people are aware of its connection to White or Washington's inauguration.

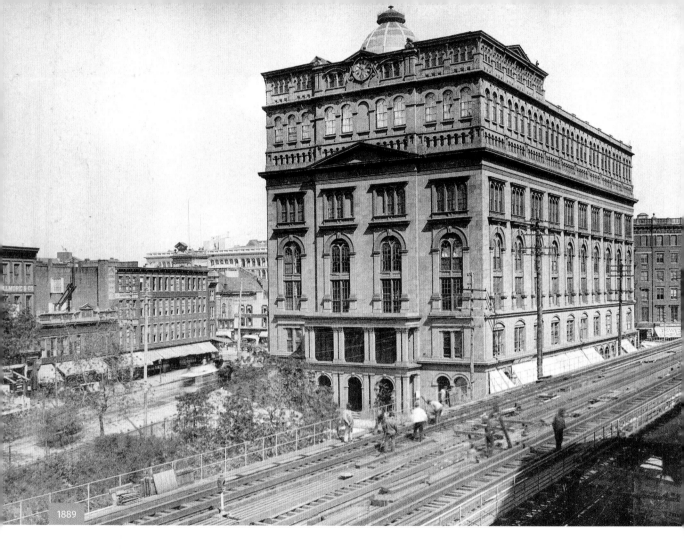

1889

COOPER UNION

A novel undertaking by an eclectic philanthropist

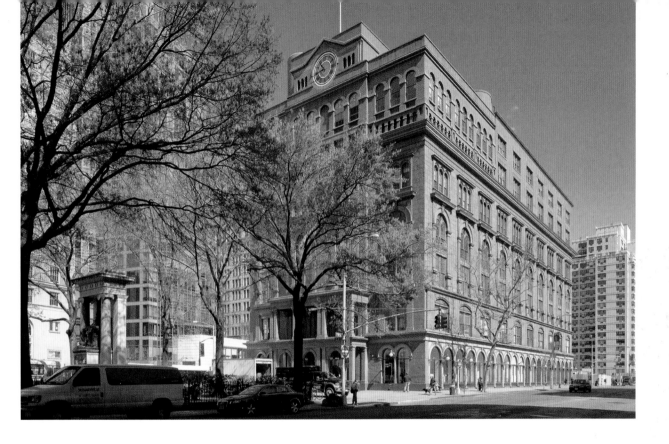

LEFT: Peter Cooper was an eclectic inventor, involved in everything from laying the Atlantic telegraph cable to producing edible gelatin, later known as Jell-O. Highly successful, but with little formal education, he established this building on Astor Place and East Eighth Street in 1859 as the Cooper Union for the Advancement of Science and Art, seen here in 1889. It was a novel undertaking, offering the first free, nonsectarian education to men and women of the working class. And it was a unique engineering achievement, using a framework of steel railroad beams from Cooper's foundry.

ABOVE: True to its founder's wishes, Cooper Union still offers students full-tuition scholarships to study architecture, fine arts, or engineering. The school is one of the highest-rated colleges in the country, and its Greenwich Village location, just east of Washington Square, has become one of the most desirable neighborhoods in the city. The elevated tracks in the earlier photo came down in 1959, opening the building to more light and air. It is the nation's oldest standing building framed with steel beams. The glass apartment tower built across the street from the school in 2005 (left) was designed by the architect Charles Gwathmey, whose father taught painting at Cooper Union for many years.

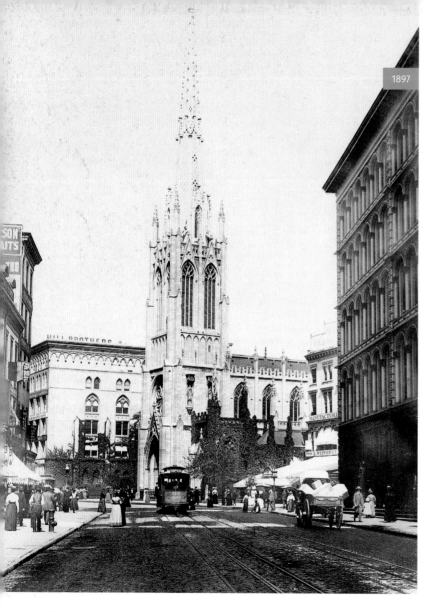

1897

GRACE CHURCH

A bump in the street grid was an opportunity for an outstanding design

LEFT: Located on a bend in Broadway, Grace Church stands out in this 1897 photo. It owes its prominent position to the stubbornness of a farmer who held onto his land when the city was laying out the street grid in 1811. Built in 1846, the graceful Gothic Revival church was designed by James Renwick years before he created the better known St. Patrick's Cathedral uptown. Partially visible on the right is a department store erected by A. T. Stewart in 1862. A cast-iron palace, it took up an entire block on Broadway between Ninth and Tenth Streets. After Stewart died in 1876, the store lost business, but by the time of this photo, it was under new management. John Wanamaker bought it in 1896, built a magnificent addition on Eighth Street, and for the next half century made Wanamaker's the ultimate name in merchandising.

BELOW: Wanamaker's Department Store in 1903, a cast-iron palace across the street from Grace Church.

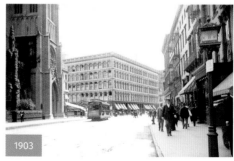

1903

RIGHT: Grace Church is widely recognized as an architectural treasure. But Wanamaker's was destroyed in a spectacular fire that burned for two days in 1956. The apartment building that replaced it, behind the trees to the right, is appropriately named Stewart House for the original building's first owner. Wanamaker's addition, not visible in this photo, is still across the street on Wanamaker Place. It is now home to K-Mart, the first New York City branch of this largely suburban chain of discount stores. The tower to the right of the church steeple was built on top of the Con Ed Building on Fourteenth Street in 1926 to commemorate the lives lost in World War I.

BELOW: Looking south from Grace Church toward the Stewart House apartment building that replaced the original Wanamaker's Department Store.

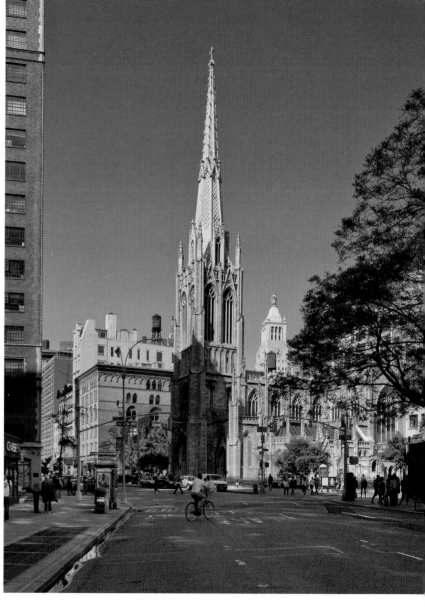

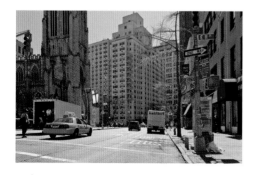

UNION SQUARE EAST

A park made famous by political demonstrators
and contemporary foodies

BELOW: Known for its workers' rallies and mass political protests, Union Square's history is closely tied to the rise of the labor movement. On September 5, 1882, some 10,000 workers paraded through the square in the nation's first Labor Day celebration. But the site's name actually comes from its location at the union of two major roads, Broadway and Fourth Avenue. In this 1905 photo, the equestrian statue of George Washington, erected in 1856, is in the middle of Fourth Avenue at Fourteenth Street on the east side of the square. Three years later, on March 28, 1908, an anarchist set off a bomb in the square, killing himself and one other man. Socialists and suffragettes also held rallies here in the early twentieth century.

c. 1905

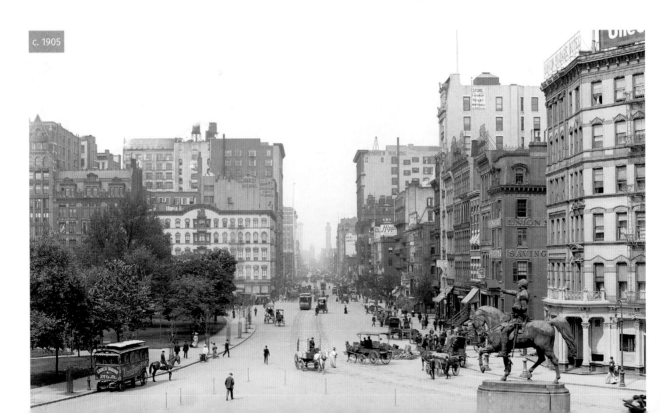

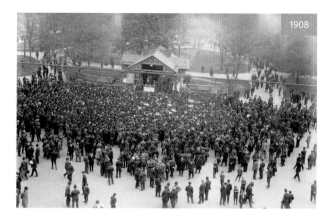

LEFT: A socialist rally in the square in 1908. As many as a million workers congregated here each May Day in the early 1900s.

BELOW: Since its early history, Union Square Park has gone through several transformations. It was completely demolished in 1928–29 to make way for a large underground subway concourse. It reemerged in 1930 with a new landscape and the statue of George Washington relocated within the park. Shabby and overrun by drug dealers in the 1970s, the park was completely refurbished in the 1980s and became a lively attraction as the home of New York's first (and now largest) farmers' market. The popular market has led to a boom in gourmet restaurants on the surrounding blocks. The statue of Washington was moved and now presides over the southern end of the park.

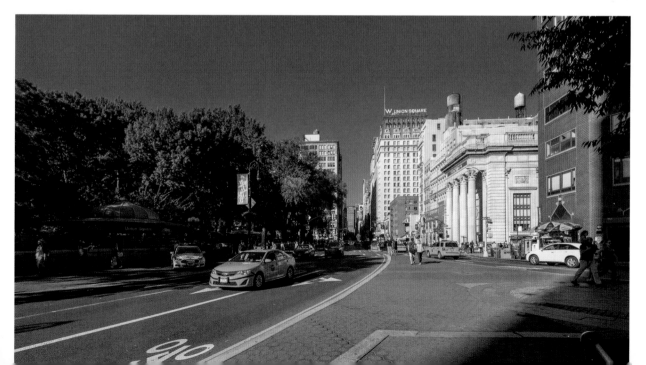

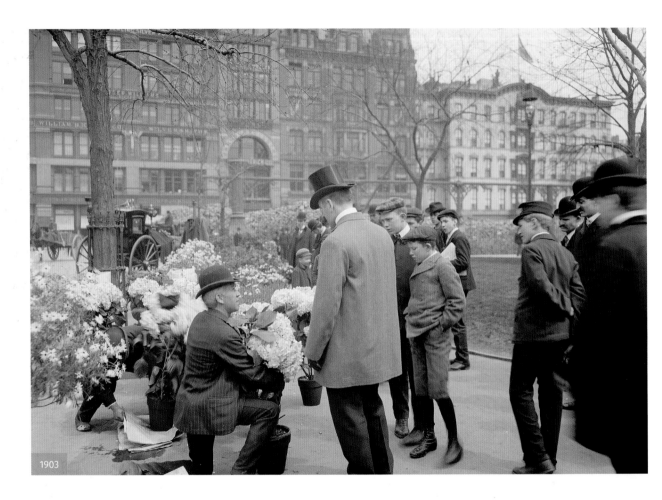

1903

UNION SQUARE NORTH

Generations of flower vendors have flocked
to the square

LEFT: Although fashionable townhouses surrounded Union Square in the mid-nineteenth century, by the time of this photo, the neighborhood had been a bustling commercial and entertainment center for several decades. The activity made Union Square a good place to do business, especially in holiday seasons, when the Easter flower market shown here was a popular attraction. The large building in the background is the Century Company Building. Completed in 1881 on the north end of the square, it was first leased to the publishers of the popular *Century* and *St. Nicholas* magazines.

BELOW: Flower vendors drove their horse-drawn wagons directly into the northern end of the square. This view is looking toward Union Square West and Seventeenth Street (right).

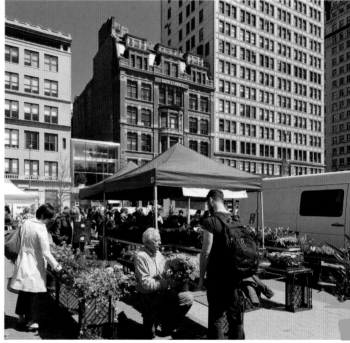

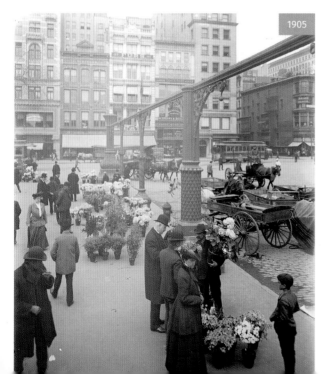

ABOVE: Just as they did a century ago, vendors are selling flowers in Union Square. But they are now part of the largest farmers' market in the city, selling a bounty of fresh vegetables, meats, baked goods, and many other edibles produced within a day's drive of the city. The Century Company Building, the only survivor from the archival image, has been reduced to a fraction of its original size. Nonetheless, it has been a comfortable space for a Barnes & Noble bookstore for many years, an appropriate transition for a building first home to magazine publishers. The Decker Building, shown on the left side of the 1905 photo, housed Andy Warhol's Factory from 1968 to 1973. In 1968, the radical feminist writer Valerie Solanas entered the sixth floor studio and shot Warhol, nearly killing him.

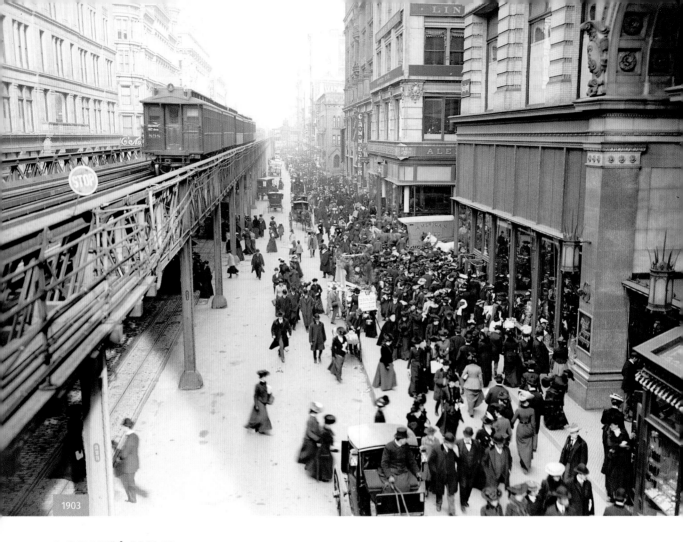

1903

LADIES' MILE

Lavish department stores have become
well-known chain stores

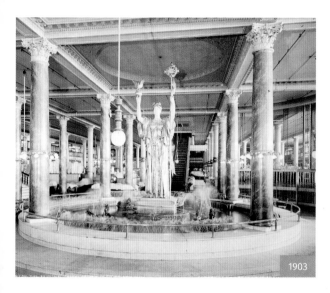

1903

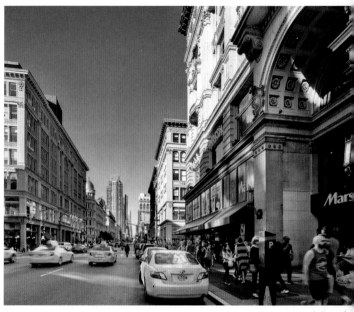

LEFT: Department stores aimed at luring women shoppers began in the mid-nineteenth century when major retailers built palatial marble and cast-iron showplaces along Sixth Avenue and Broadway between Union and Madison Squares. The booming economy after the Civil War created a new demographic of affluent shoppers, mostly upper-middle-class women, who were moving uptown. Macy's opened its first store at Union Square on Fourteenth Street and Sixth Avenue in 1858. In 1878, elevated train tracks went up on Sixth Avenue, drawing even more shoppers to what became known as the Ladies' Mile. The main attraction, opened in 1896, was the store on the right, Siegel-Cooper's huge, elaborate emporium at Eighteenth Street. Calling itself the "Big Store—a City in Itself" and covering fifteen acres, it offered "everything under the sun," drawing 150,000 shoppers on its opening day.

ABOVE: Inside Siegel-Cooper's, a lavish fountain welcomed shoppers to the store. It was modeled on the famous fountain at the 1893 World's Fair in Chicago, where "meet me at the fountain" was a well-known refrain.

ABOVE: Macy's moved up to Thirty-fourth Street in 1903, replacing Siegel-Cooper's as the "world's largest department store." The other big stores on the Ladies' Mile—Lord & Taylor, B. Altman, W. & J. Sloane, Best & Company, and Bergdorf-Goodman, everyone except Siegel-Cooper—eventually moved uptown. By World War I, the company declared bankruptcy and it became a military hospital during the war, and then a warehouse. Along with the other grand stores of the Ladies' Mile, the building fell into disrepair and the area remained marginal even after the elevated tracks came down in the 1940s. In the 1980s, architects, photographers, advertising firms, and other cutting-edge businesses were attracted by the low rents and spacious buildings. The area was declared a historic district in 1989, ensuring that its architectural features would be preserved. Siegel-Cooper's is once again a "Big Store," filled with goods from several national chains.

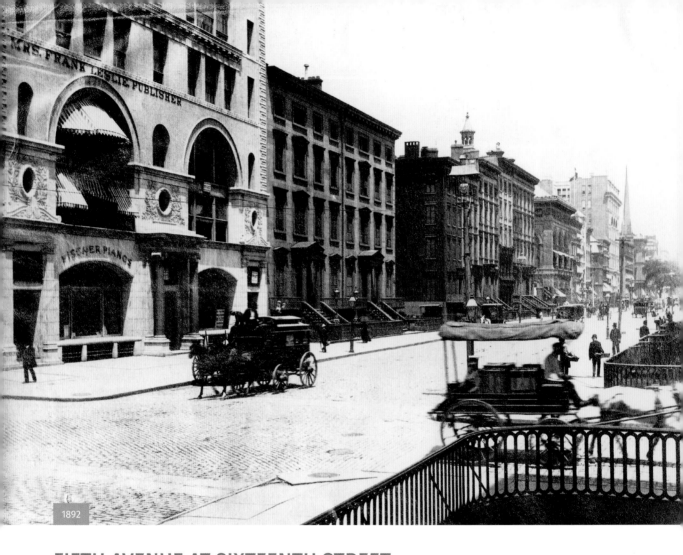

1892

FIFTH AVENUE AT SIXTEENTH STREET

A female pioneer in publishing built her headquarters here

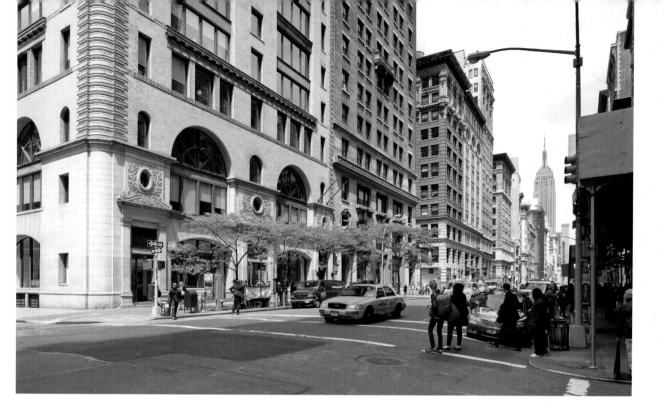

LEFT: A close look at the writing on the large corner building in this 1892 photo reveals two popular aspects of late nineteenth-century entertainment. Over the ground floor entrance is the name, Fischer Pianos, a producer of high-quality pianos much in demand by America's rising middle class. Above the central arched window is the name of the publisher of the country's most widely read weekly magazine, *Frank Leslie's Illustrated Newspaper.* Launched in 1855 as the first of its kind in the country, the publication was an enormous success, until the depression of the 1870s. After Leslie's death in 1880, his wife, Miriam, brought the business back to profitability—hence the name Mrs. Frank Leslie on the building. She commissioned the architectural firm of McKim, Mead and White to build it in 1890.

ABOVE: Although hundreds of American piano companies flourished in the nineteenth century, few survive today, but Fischer Piano was one of the longest in operation, from 1840 to 1982. Frank Leslie's publications no longer exist. Miriam Leslie died in 1914 and left an estate valued at $2 million to the women's suffrage movement. The arched facade of her building, destroyed in the 1970s, has been beautifully restored. Every other building in the older photo has been replaced, and the Empire State Building now rises in the background.

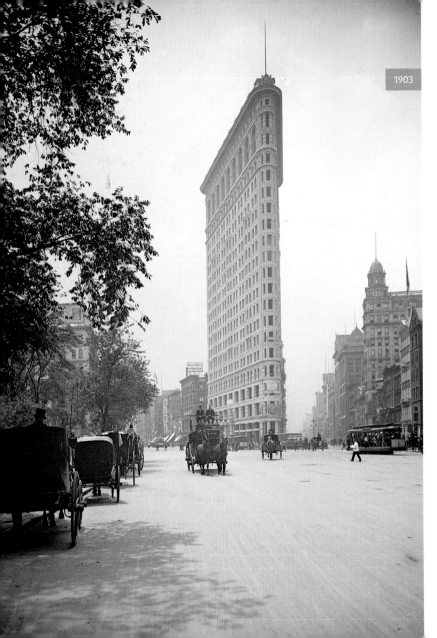

1903

FLATIRON BUILDING
Criticized as a folly, it became an architectural icon

LEFT: Rising like the prow of a great ship, the Flatiron Building was the first tall structure to soar north of City Hall. Built on a triangular island on Twenty-third Street between Fifth Avenue and Broadway, it literally stood out on its own. As the only building on the site, it appeared much taller than its twenty-three stories. Seen here just south of Madison Square Park (left) in 1903, the year of its completion, it was called the Fuller Building, but soon became identified by its flatiron shape. Although it was built with a steel skeleton, its undulating brick-and-terra-cotta facade created a ripple effect, making the building shimmer in changing light. It was designed by Daniel Burnham, a Chicago-based architect. At the time of its completion, the public, still wary of skyscrapers, feared that it would topple, and called it "Burnham's Folly."

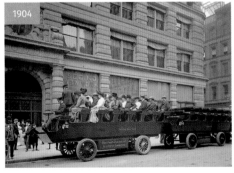

1904

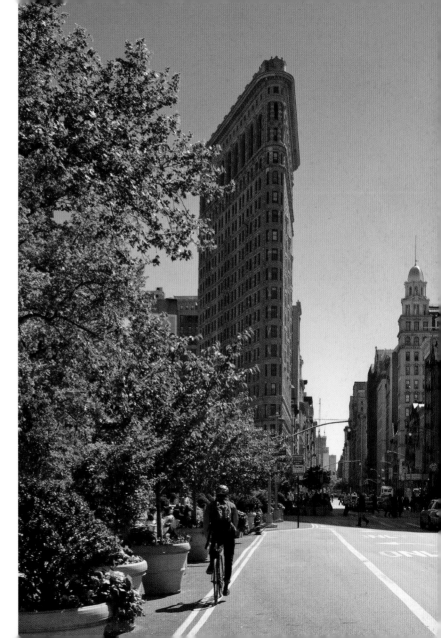

RIGHT: Surrounded today by tall buildings, the Flatiron's solitary stance on a triangular island still sets it apart and makes it one of New York City's most recognizable landmarks. It has also become part of a trendy neighborhood, called the Flatiron District. Located between Madison Square Park and Chelsea, the district is filled with restaurants and condo apartments converted from old office buildings. Famous photos of the Flatiron Building by Edward Steichen and Alfred Stieglitz captured the public's imagination, then and now. Unencumbered by the changes around it, the Flatiron remains one of New York City's most romantic symbols.

LEFT: This sightseeing bus boarded passengers at the entrance to the Flatiron Building, a place every tourist wanted to see.

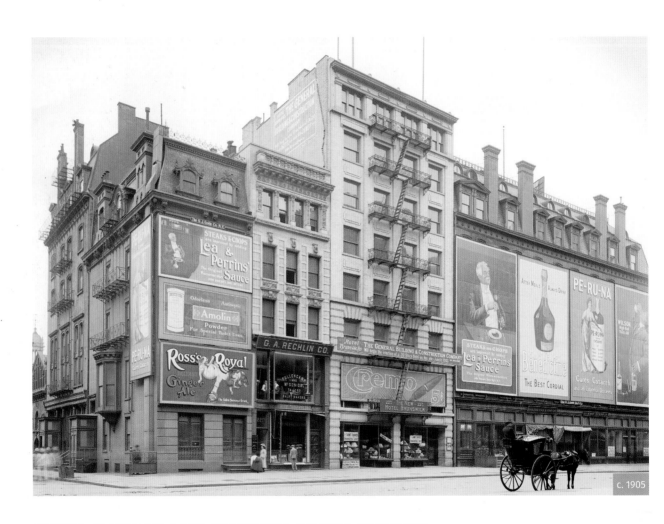
c. 1905

FIFTH AVENUE AND TWENTY-SIXTH STREET

The photography company located here left a legacy of historic images

LEFT: This block just above Madison Square Park was once the neighborhood of writer Edith Wharton, but by the time of this early 1900s photo, the march of commercialization had reached the once-elegant area. The giant billboards cover most of the row houses that had been fashionable Fifth Avenue homes. Thanks to a small storefront within the block (second from the left), this photo and countless more still provide century-old images of New York City that otherwise might have vanished. The storefront, at 229 Fifth Avenue, was the office of the Detroit Photographic Company, which sold millions of prints each year, including many of the archival images in this book. Launched in the late 1890s by a Detroit businessman, the company became one of the largest American publishers of postcards and photographs in the early decades of the twentieth century, with sales offices in New York City, Los Angeles, Detroit, London, and Zurich. The photo below shows the interior of the Detroit Publishing Company's Fifth Avenue office.

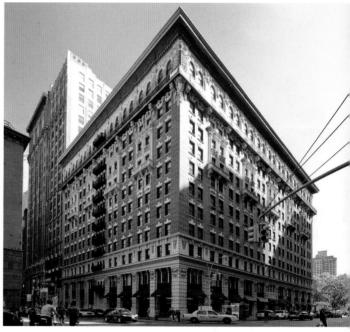

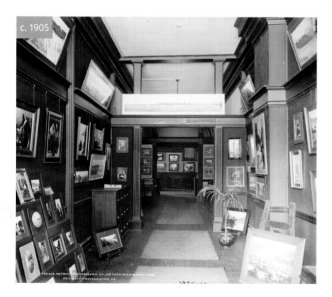

c. 1905

ABOVE: It is not often that the city's nineteenth-century buildings give way to more distinctive architecture. But in this case, the large building that now stands on this site is an elegant replacement for the row houses. Built in 1906 as the Brunswick Hotel, it is now the Grand Madison, filled with expensive condos. The Detroit Photographic Company came to an end in the 1920s, but also left a valuable legacy. After World War I, the company was hurt by cheaper printing methods used by its competitors. It went bankrupt in 1924, and its assets were liquidated in 1932. Fortunately, the company manager gave all the negatives and prints to the Edison Institute in Dearborn, Michigan. They were transferred in 1949 to the Colorado Historical Society, which gave them to the Library of Congress, where they are now available to the public.

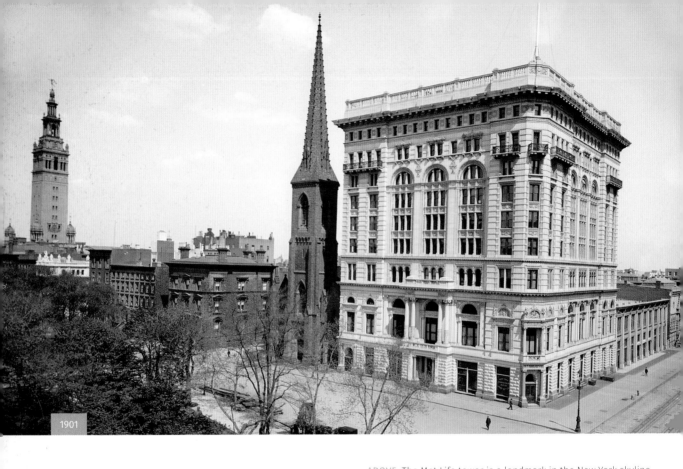

1901

METROPOLITAN LIFE BUILDING

The company's headquarters evolved from
modest beginnings to a megalith

ABOVE: The Met Life tower is a landmark in the New York skyline,
but this 1901 photo is a little-known view of its modest origins.
The original nine-story building, shown here without its tower, was
constructed in 1892 on the corner of Madison Avenue and Twenty-
third Street. It stands next to the Madison Avenue Presbyterian
Church, a Gothic edifice from the mid-nineteenth century. Eight
years after this photo was taken, the scene changed dramatically.
The church next door came down, and the fifty-story Met Life
tower rose in 1909, a virtual replica—on a gigantic scale—of the
Campanile in St. Mark's Square in Venice.

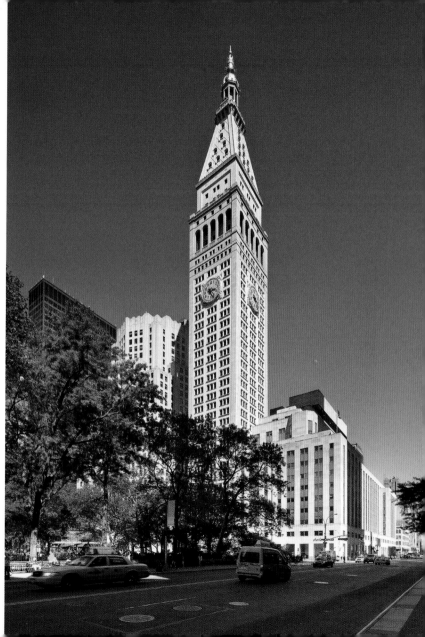

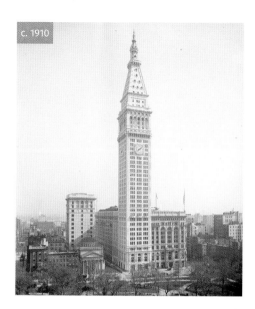

c. 1910

ABOVE: The Met Life tower on the same site previously occupied by the church. The new church with a domed roof is across the street.

RIGHT: The Met Life Building lost its glory in 1964. The original base was replaced by a twelve-story box, but the real damage was done to the tower. Stripped of its ornament to give it a "more modern look," it became a mere warehouse for company records, in effect, a skyscraper attic. But it still puts on a good show. Met Life's motto, "The Light that Never Fails," is an ironic postscript for the building that was abandoned by its company, yet the tower, illuminated by floodlights, still lights up the skyline. After a long restoration, the building was converted to a luxury hotel that opened in 2015.

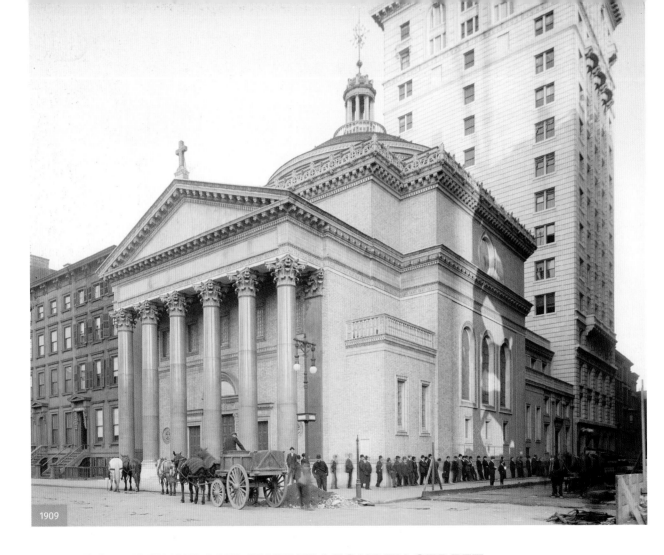

1909

MADISON AVENUE AND TWENTY-FOURTH STREET

A church swallowed by corporate expansion

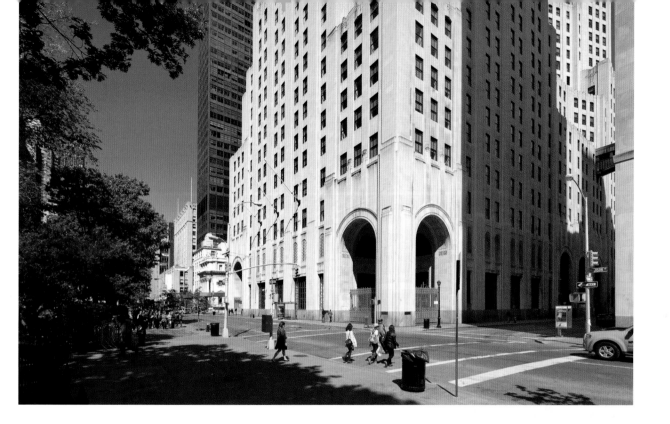

LEFT: After the original Madison Avenue Presbyterian Church was demolished to make way for the Met Life Tower, this church was built as its replacement, directly across Twenty-fourth Street. The church minister, Dr. Charles Parkhurst, encouraged the architect, Stanford White, to develop a less-austere design than the Gothic original. Completed in 1906, the new church, more like ancient Rome than the Middle Ages, was a staunch response to the tower scheduled to rise three years later across the street. The men lined up along the church seem to be watching the tower construction, and some signs of it can be seen in the far right corner.

ABOVE: The new church was widely acclaimed, but lasted only thirteen years. Met Life's insurance empire was growing rapidly, and the company was eyeing the church site for another building. In 1919, the church was taken apart piece by piece. Although the plan was to rebuild it on another site, one was never found. Not content with the building that replaced the church, Met Life planned to build another tower on the same site in 1929, this one to reach 100 stories. The ambitious plan was halted by the Depression, and only the tower's base was built, as seen above. Taking up the entire block, it includes monumental arcades and lobbies. Planned to accommodate an army of clerks, it never got above thirty-odd stories.

MACY'S

The "world's largest department store"

BELOW: In this 1905 photo, Macy's had just opened its doors on Herald Square at Thirty-fourth Street and Sixth Avenue. Rowland Hussey "R. H." Macy had opened the store in 1858 on Union Square, but did not live to see it rise to its full glory. The men behind the move uptown were the new owners and innovative entrepreneurs, Isidor and Nathan Straus. They built this huge emporium on the site of Oscar Hammerstein's Manhattan Opera House, which moved further uptown to establish a new theater district on Forty-second Street and Broadway. The Strauses failed to gain control of the entire site, as seen by the small corner building nestled within Macy's embrace. The owner, Siegel-Cooper, held out for an exorbitant sum, so the Strauses simply built around it.

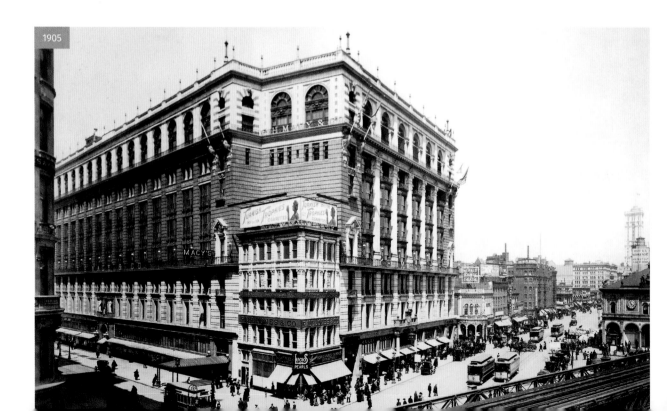

1905

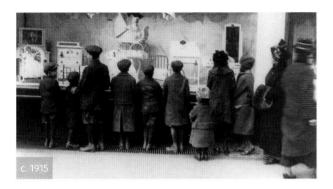

c. 1915

BELOW: Today, Macy's famous sign covers the corner building that the Straus brothers failed to acquire. Descendants of the original owner still control the little building and lease the facade to Macy's. The star trademark harks back to the founder, R. H. Macy, a onetime whaler who, legend has it, got the idea from his tattoo. The first big department store to move far north of Union Square, Macy's made Herald Square the city's busiest shopping district. It also made the Strauses a fortune, but nine years after launching the store, Isidor and his wife died on the *Titanic*. Although she was offered a place on a lifeboat, she would not leave her husband to die alone.

LEFT: Children gaze at Macy's Christmas toy window display.

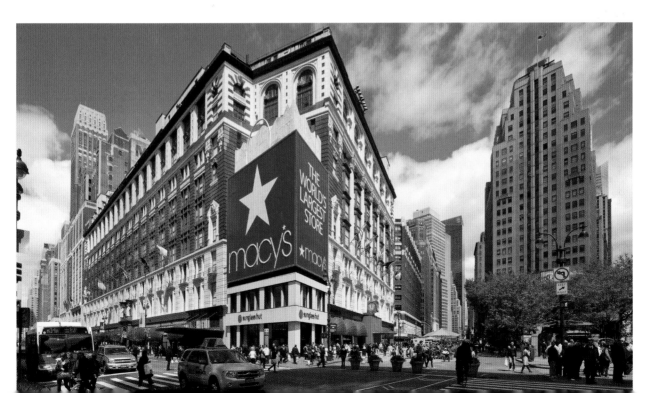

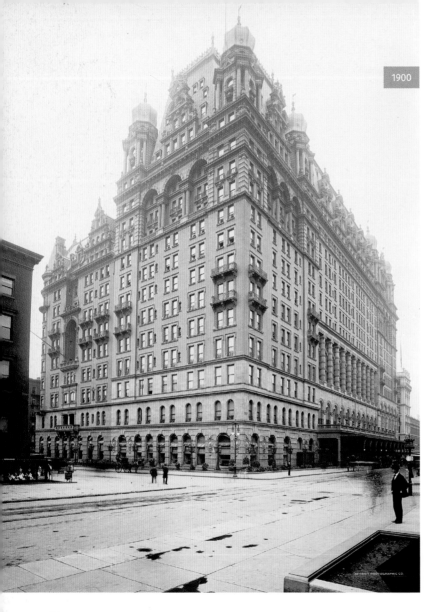

FIFTH AVENUE AND THIRTY-FOURTH STREET

The city's grandest hotel gave way to one of its tallest buildings

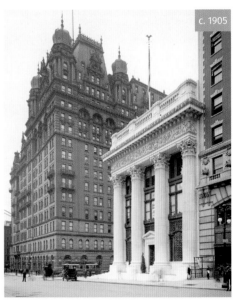

ABOVE: Looking south toward the hotel from Fifth Avenue and Thirty-fourth Street, this view also shows the Knickerbocker Trust Bank with its grand columned facade. Built in 1904, the bank was one of Stanford White's greatest designs. Unfortunately, the bank's owner, like White, ended his life in scandal. After his multimillion-dollar loans went bad in 1906, he committed suicide.

OPPOSITE: The first Waldorf-Astoria was originally two side-by-side hotels built by feuding cousins of the Astor family. William Waldorf Astor built the first one, the Hotel Waldorf, in 1893, overshadowing the neighboring mansion of his despised aunt Caroline. Her son, John Jacob Astor, at first planned to demolish his mother's house and build stables to stink up his cousin's opulent hotel. But since their fortunes were tied together, John Jacob reconsidered and instead built the Astoria in 1897, an even larger, more splendid building. The two buildings functioned as one hotel, but the cousins agreed that if their alliance fell apart, they could seal off the ground-floor connection. Their success was so great that it never happened. Seen here in 1900, the Waldorf-Astoria was the city's grandest hotel and New York society's favorite place to dine, dance, and drink. This view is looking north from Thirty-third Street and Fifth Avenue.

RIGHT: As society moved further uptown, the original Waldorf-Astoria died of thirst during Prohibition and was demolished in 1928 to make way for the Empire State Building. Both the Empire State and the new Waldorf-Astoria Hotel, a streamlined sophisticate on Park Avenue and Fiftieth Street, were completed in 1931. The Empire State broke all construction records, reaching 102 stories in fifteen months. Opened at the start of the Great Depression, it had no rivals for height, but plenty of competition for office space. For years it was called "the Empty State" and survived on entrance fees to its lofty observation deck. It was the city's tallest building until the north tower of the World Trade Center reached 110 stories in 1972.

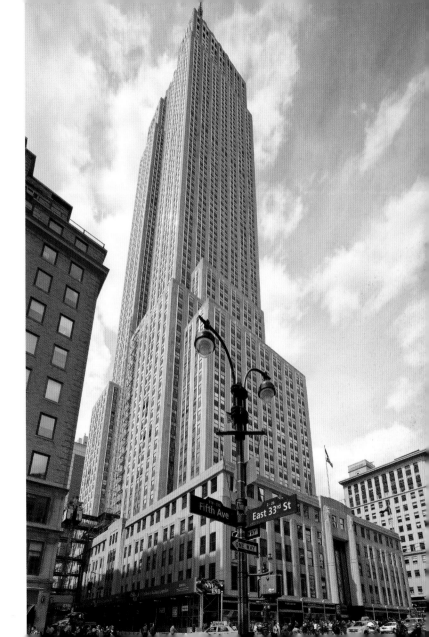

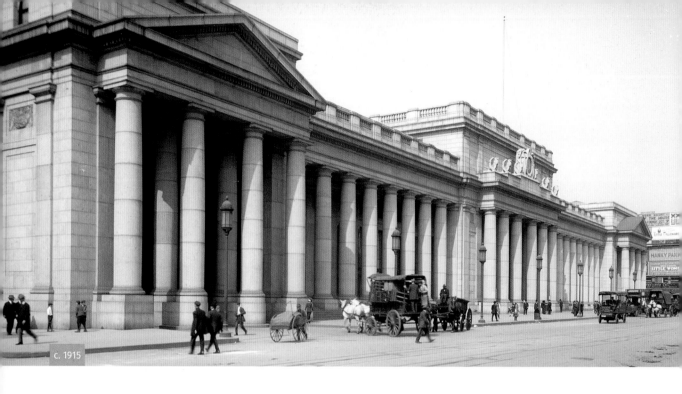

c. 1915

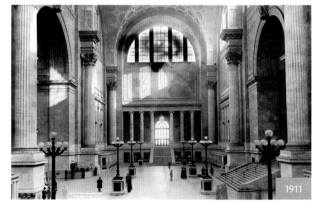

1911

PENN STATION

A monument of civic architecture replaced
by a building shaped like a giant doughnut

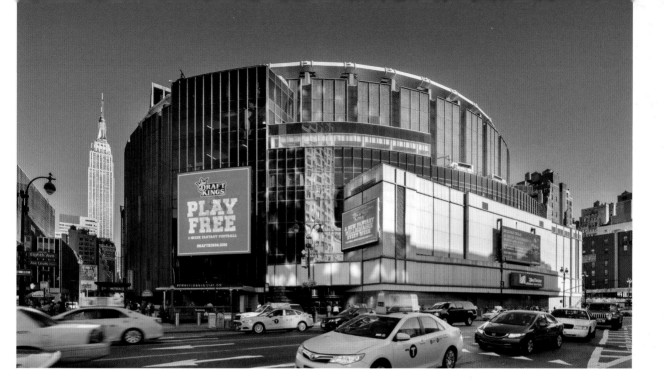

ABOVE LEFT: This monumental, two-block-long classical temple was built between 1904 and 1910. To build its first station in New York City, the Pennsylvania Railroad cut a tunnel under the Hudson River in 1904, connecting the island of Manhattan to the rest of the country. Like Grand Central, the city's other great train station in construction at this time, Penn Station was an engineering and architectural marvel. Designed by McKim, Mead and White, construction of the station cleared blocks of tenements in Hell's Kitchen and was heralded as the dawning of a new era for West Midtown.

ABOVE: Like the tenements it replaced, Penn Station fell victim to changing times and property values. As automobiles outpaced train service in the 1960s, the railroad sacrificed its grand station to higher real estate revenues. Demolition began in 1963, replacing the station in 1968 with an office tower and the new Madison Square Garden, a giant doughnut of a building dropped on the site of the grand waiting room. To sports and rock-concert fans, the Garden is the ultimate venue. To those who remember the original Penn Station, however, the modern building is a sad reminder of the loss of a magnificent space. Its loss led to a public outcry and the creation of the city's first landmark protection law in 1965.

LEFT: The main waiting room, seen here in 1911, a year after the station's completion, was an awe-inspiring space.

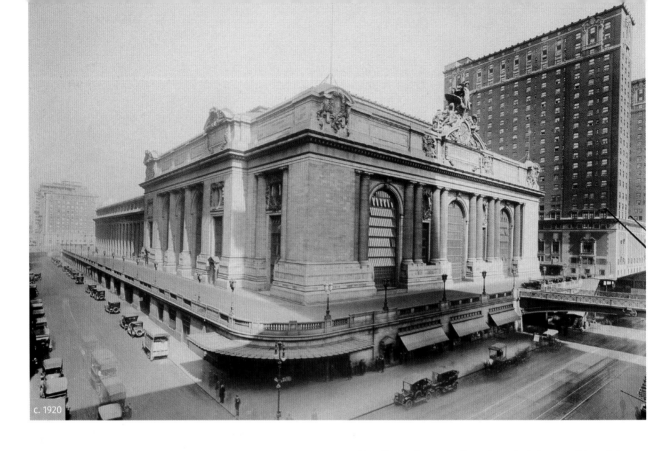

c. 1920

GRAND CENTRAL

Built as a grand gateway to the city, the terminal led to New York's expansion

ABOVE: Elevated on a platform above Park Avenue with a triple-arched facade, Grand Central Terminal was built as a gateway to New York City. Completed in 1913, it replaced the first Grand Central Depot built here at Forty-second Street in 1871, when that street was at the northern end of the city. The new terminal, the crowning glory of Cornelius Vanderbilt's New York Central Railroad, brought several railroad lines together under one roof and spearheaded the city's expansion beyond Forty-second Street. The taller building on the right is the Commodore Hotel, built in 1919 by Vanderbilt, who was known as the "Commodore" for his first career in shipping lines.

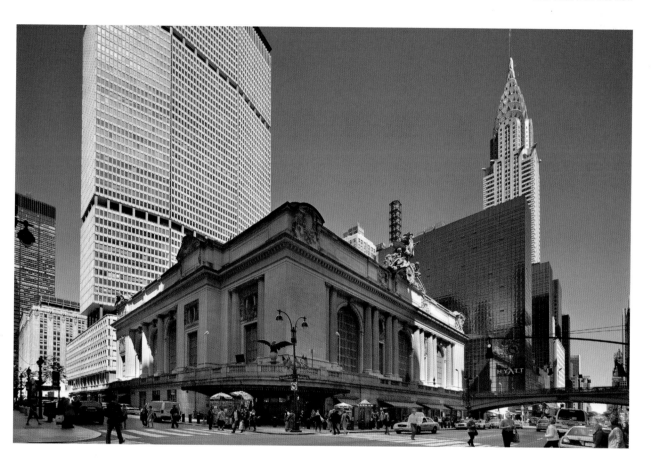

ABOVE: Over the years, Grand Central Terminal was surrounded by much taller buildings. Behind it is a glass slab built in the 1960s as the Pan Am Building, now the Met Life Building. Critics called it "a monstrous bland blanket." In the late 1970s, the railroad and the Commodore Hotel were on the brink of bankruptcy. Donald Trump bought the hotel and reopened it as the glass-sheathed Grand Hyatt in 1980. Ever since the 1950s, the financially strapped railroad had been trying to demolish or drastically alter the building. Preservationists fought to save it and, after a long court battle, finally prevailed in 1978. The eagle perched above the corner entrance was salvaged from the less fortunate Penn Station. The sleek Chrysler Building stands like a sentinel on the far right.

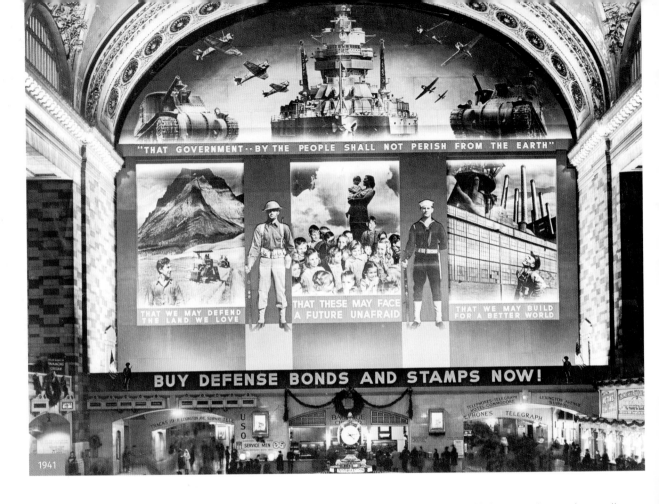

"THAT GOVERNMENT · BY THE PEOPLE SHALL NOT PERISH FROM THE EARTH"

THAT WE MAY DEFEND THE LAND WE LOVE

THAT THESE MAY FACE A FUTURE UNAFRAID

THAT WE MAY BUILD FOR A BETTER WORLD

BUY DEFENSE BONDS AND STAMPS NOW!

1941

GRAND CENTRAL

A wartime mural foreshadowed a period of decline for the terminal

ABOVE: During World War II, this huge mural covered one wall of Grand Central's towering windows, urging the thousands who passed through to focus on the prodigious war effort. The splendid interior had been designed as a superb embodiment of the terminal's monumental character. Towering columns rose to a vaulted ceiling painted with a mural of the constellations. Spotlights behind the ceiling illuminated the stars.

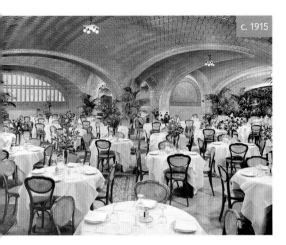

c. 1915

ABOVE AND BELOW: Grand Central's Oyster Bar and Restaurant, with its distinctive ceiling embellished with Guastavino tiles, began operating when the terminal opened in 1913.

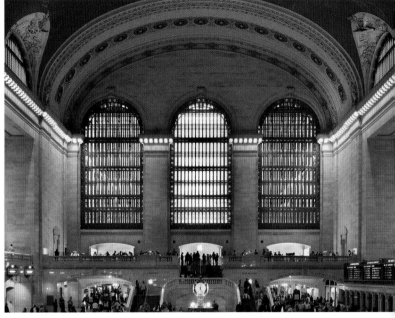

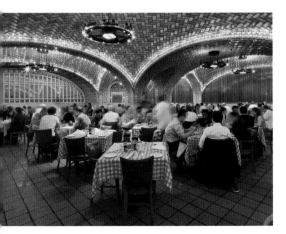

ABOVE: The main concourse is a glorious space today, thanks to a decades-long preservation battle that saved the terminal from destruction. With train service declining in the 1950s, the ceiling lights of the zodiac went out, grime stained the stone columns, and a giant screen advertising Kodak film covered the wall of grand windows. At first, the railroad tried to demolish the terminal and, when that failed, tried to build a skyscraper on top of it that would have pierced this room with steel columns. In 1978, after years of lawsuits, the U.S. Supreme Court upheld the terminal's landmark protection. Twenty years later, the Kodak screen finally came down, a marble staircase went up in its place, the cerulean blue ceiling was cleaned, and its stars were lit once again. Filled with bustling shops and restaurants, the concourse is now a vibrant place for tens of thousands of commuters.

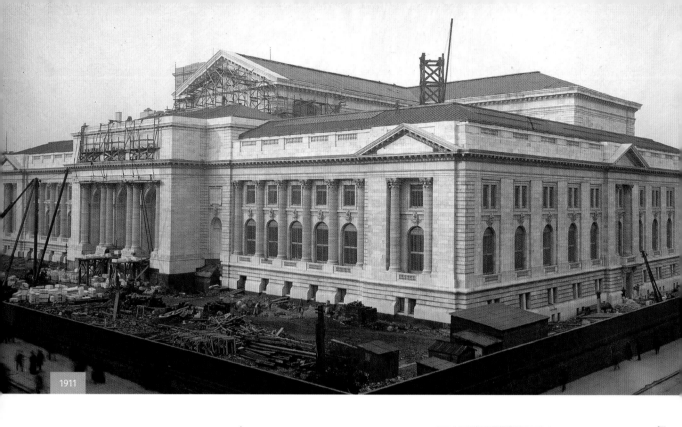

1911

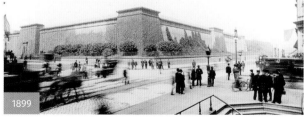

1899

NEW YORK PUBLIC LIBRARY

Operating for a century, the library receives
sixteen million visitors each year

ABOVE: The 1842 reservoir that previously stood on the library site
distributed water piped in from the Croton watershed forty miles north
of the city.

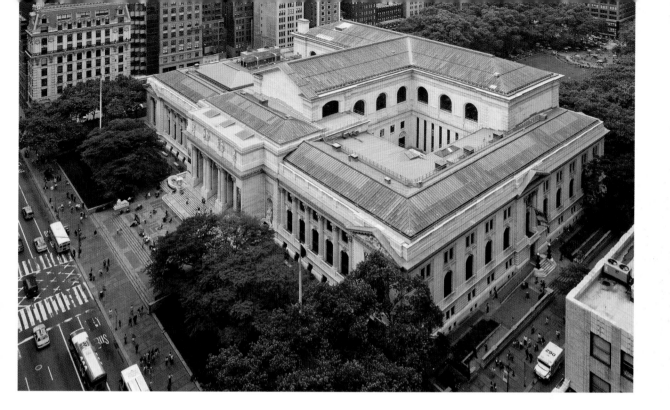

ABOVE LEFT: Nearly complete in 1911, the New York Public Library was the largest marble structure ever built in the United States. It covered two blocks on Fifth Avenue between Fortieth and Forty-second Streets, previously the site of the vast Croton Reservoir. It took 500 men working two years to dismantle the reservoir. The cornerstone was laid in 1902, but work progressed slowly on building the monumental structure. The books were donated by the Astor and Lenox libraries, two of the city's largest private collections. The idea of a free public library had been the wish of former New York governor Samuel J. Tilden, who, at his death in 1886, bequeathed the bulk of his $2.4 million fortune to endow the project. Steel baron Andrew Carnegie provided another $5.2 million to fund a citywide system of associated neighborhood libraries.

ABOVE: On opening day, May 24, 1911, between 30,000 and 50,000 people streamed through the main library. It became an essential part of the city's intellectual life, helping to educate New Yorkers and recently arrived immigrants. Isaac Bashevis Singer, Norman Mailer, E. L. Doctorow, and many other New York–based authors and scholars did research here. Private donors came together again in the 1980s and 1990s to restore the building to its original splendor. A unique facility today, it includes fifty million items in its research and circulating collections, shared by eighty-five branch libraries. Sixteen million people visit the main library each year. The famous stone lions at the library steps, dubbed Patience and Fortitude by Mayor Fiorello La Guardia in the 1930s, have been at their posts since the building opened over a century ago.

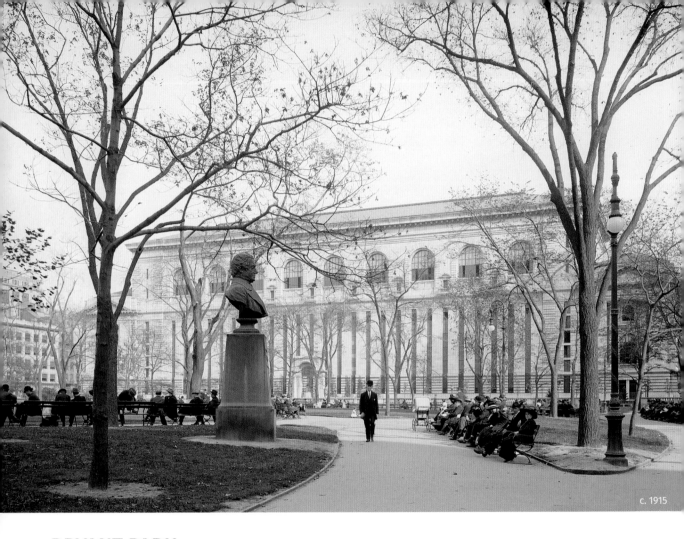

c. 1915

BRYANT PARK

Before it was a park, this was the site of a world's
fair and a brutal Civil War–era mob riot

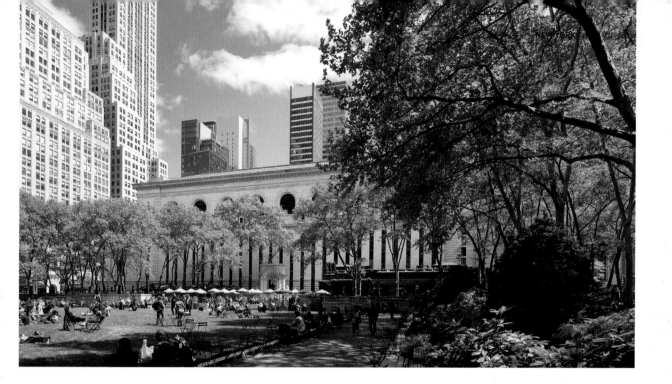

LEFT: The New York Public Library, seen here from its rear western side, was still new in this early twentieth-century photo. Its backyard had been a public park for more than fifty years, although it had served many different purposes. In 1853, it was the site of the Crystal Palace, an enormous glass-and-iron building inspired by London's famous exhibition hall of 1851. The first of its kind in New York City, the Crystal Palace drew more than one million visitors, but closed the following year and burned down in 1858. During the Civil War, Union army troops camped on the site, and in the draft riots of 1863, it was overrun by brutal mobs that burned down a nearby orphanage on Fifth Avenue and Forty-third Street. In 1871, the area finally became a more traditional park, similar to the one seen here. It was renamed Bryant Park in 1884 to honor the journalist and abolitionist William Cullen Bryant, one of the first advocates for the creation of Central Park.

ABOVE: The park was redesigned in the 1930s with a large raised lawn and fences separating it from the adjoining streets. Cut off from its surroundings and neglected over the years, it became a drug trafficking and homeless haven, briefly interrupted by an anti–Vietnam War rally in 1969 that drew 40,000 people. Totally restored in the 1990s, it reopened to great success as a popular Midtown oasis that offers winter ice-skating, summer picnicking on the lawn, outdoor movies, and many other activities. Most of the park's visitors are unaware that millions of books are housed beneath the park in multiple layers of underground stacks.

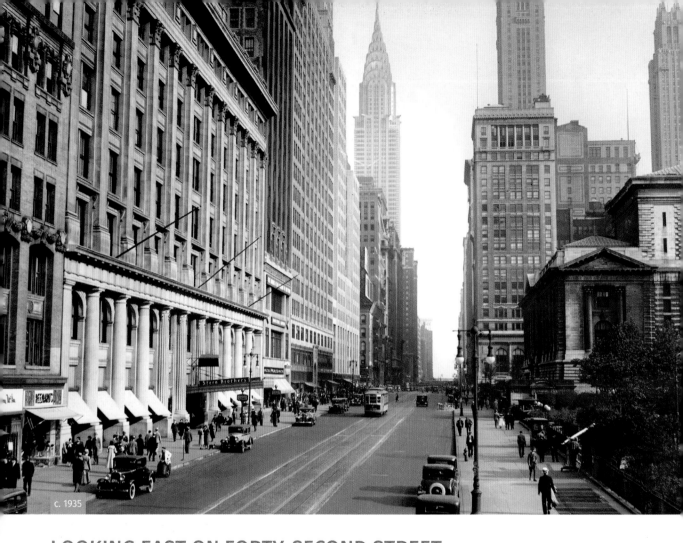

c. 1935

LOOKING EAST ON FORTY-SECOND STREET

Although the Chrysler Building's fame soared, the architect never designed another major building

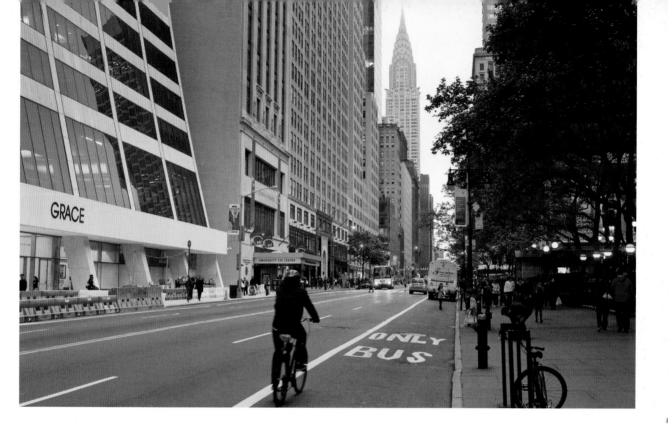

LEFT: The Art Deco spire of the Chrysler Building was a newcomer to the eastern end of Forty-second Street in 1930, the year the skyscraper won a frenzied race to become the world's tallest building. With the competing Bank of Manhattan tower at 40 Wall Street growing higher each day, Chrysler's architect, William Van Alen, hid the lancelike spire and raised it at the last minute, topping his rival by 121 feet. The victory was sweet but short-lived. The Empire State Building captured the title in 1931. This view shows Forty-second Street's older residents, the public library and Bryant Park on the right, and across the street, the columned front of the Stern Brothers department store.

ABOVE: The swooping wall of the Grace Building replaced the Stern Brothers store in 1974. The unusual form was a unique response to the city's zoning requirement to set tall buildings back from the street. By the mid-1970s, the Chrysler Building, the gleaming embodiment of the Jazz Age, had fallen on hard times. With empty offices, cracked walls, and leaks in its dome, it was sold at a bank foreclosure. Fortunately, the new owner repaired the building and in 2002 completed a total restoration, bringing the building back to its shining, showy self. Sadly, the Chrysler's architect saw his career extinguished in the 1930s. Although his work became one of the city's most beloved landmarks, Van Alen never designed another major building.

EAST MIDTOWN SKYLINE

The Chrysler Building's sleek profile stood out among its skyscraping neighbors

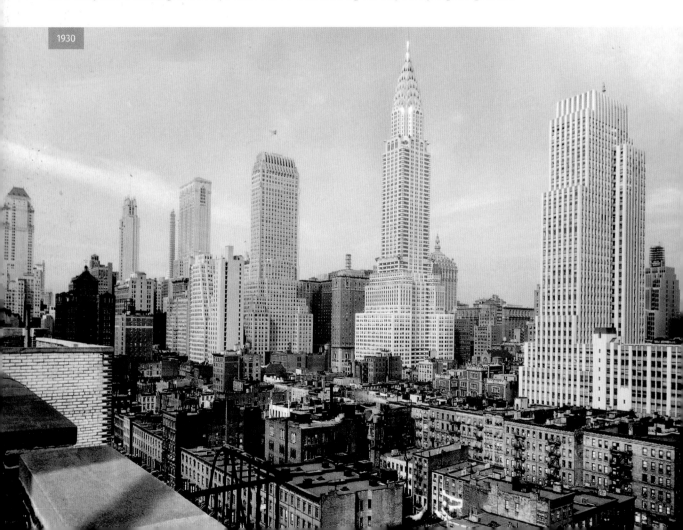

1930

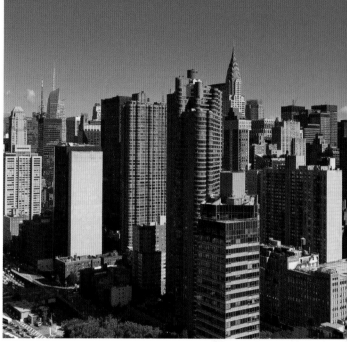

LEFT: Once the northern outskirts of the city, Forty-second Street was rivaling Wall Street as the skyscraper kingdom by the time this photo was taken in 1930. The Chrysler Building, with its unmistakable dome, had just been completed, joining a troop of towers marching up the street during the same period. To the right of the Chrysler is the Daily News Building, and to the left is the Chanin Building, both completed in 1929. Skyscrapers first appeared at Manhattan's southern tip because its narrow borders made vertical buildings an efficient way to add office space. But as tower after tower rose in Midtown—Manhattan's widest point—it became increasingly clear that efficiency was not the only incentive. Nearly every big business wanted a skyscraper to crown its success.

BELOW: *Life Magazine* photographer Margaret Bourke-White perches precariously atop a Chrysler Building gargoyle.

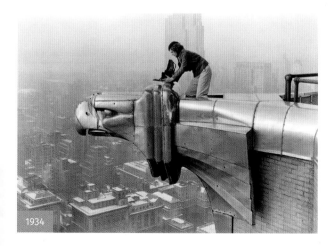

1934

ABOVE: Except for the crown of the Chrysler Building, the same view today is hardly recognizable from the older photo. Most of the other skyscrapers standing on East Forty-second Street in 1930 are still there. But over the past eight decades, many additional towers have filled the space once occupied by low-rise buildings in the foreground of the earlier shot. These newer buildings are largely residential. In East Midtown, as in many other parts of Manhattan, New Yorkers are living and working in the same densely packed neighborhoods. On the far left, the taller building with the spire is the new Bank of America Tower. Since the older shot, taken from a building roof, is now blocked by the new towers, this view was taken from a helicopter over FDR Drive.

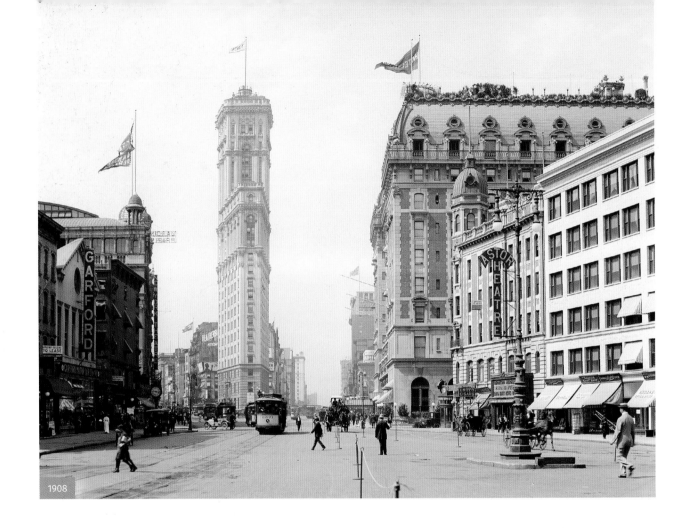

1908

TIMES TOWER

The new headquarters of the *New York Times*
launched the success of Times Square

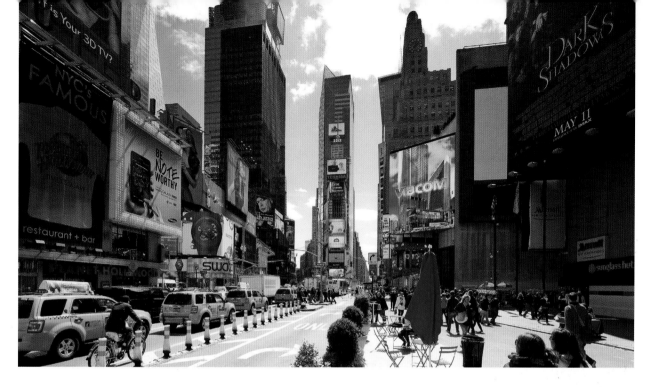

LEFT: In the center of this 1908 photo is Times Tower, the new home of the *New York Times*, which ventured uptown to the intersection of Forty-second Street, Broadway, and Seventh Avenue in 1904. The paper's old location opposite City Hall had been the nerve center of the city, but *Times* publisher Adolph Ochs knew that the new subway, which reached Forty-second Street in 1904, would bring rapid expansion to this area. Ochs convinced the subway company to name the Forty-second Street station after his paper, and the area soon became known as Times Square. On the right, the large building with the flag is the Astor Hotel, which also opened in 1904. Located on Broadway between Forty-fourth and Forty-fifth streets, it became a great success in the midst of the new Times Square theater district. Directly across the street from the Astor is Oscar Hammerstein's palatial Olympia Music Palace (1895), the first theater on Times Square.

ABOVE: A century after the *New York Times* made its daring move to a remote location, Times Square has become one of the busiest and flashiest sites in the city. Like the Times Tower itself, now covered with billboards, the area is totally transformed from the archival photo. The once-lavish Astor Hotel closed in 1967 and was replaced in 1972 by a fifty-story office building, One Astor Plaza. The Olympia Music Palace and nearly every other building in the archival shot are also gone, replaced by office buildings that dwarf Times Tower. Even the *New York Times* has left. The paper outgrew the tower by 1913 and moved to a nearby building just off the square. It moved again in 2007 to West Midtown.

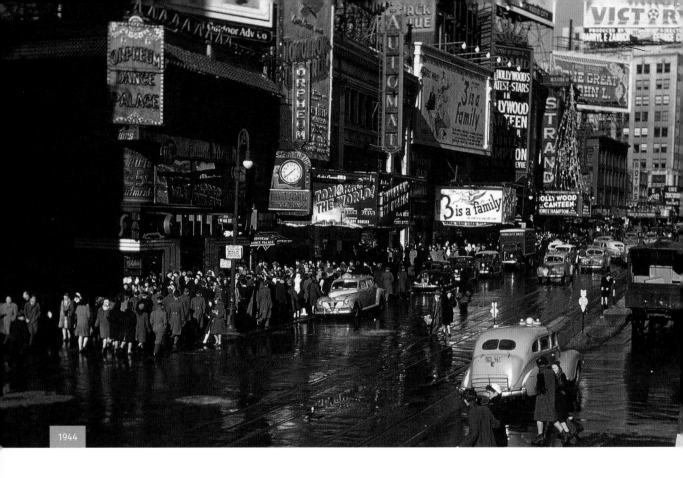

1944

TIMES SQUARE

In times of war and peace, Times Square has been the throbbing pulse of the city

ABOVE: This photo, taken in 1944, shows groups of U.S. servicemen mixed in with the Broadway crowds. Located between Forty-sixth and Forty-seventh Streets, just a few blocks north of Times Tower, this Broadway block is lined with movie theater marquees. But the lights went out at night when Times Square was part of the city's wartime blackout. Occasional air-raid drills also cleared the busy streets. Soldiers and sailors could buy a dance at the Orpheum Dance Palace (left) or get a meal for less than a dollar at the automat.

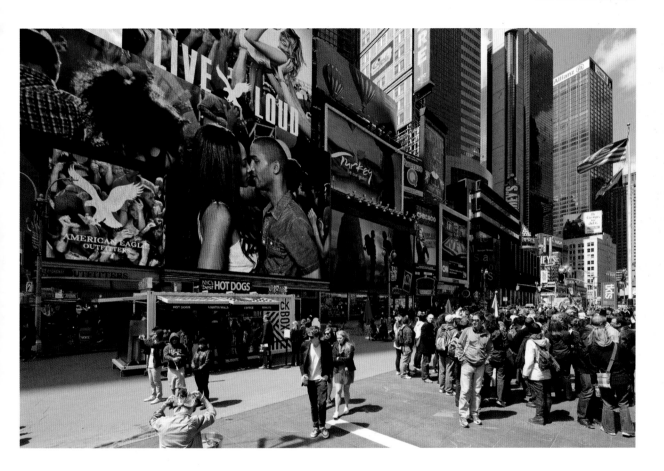

ABOVE: Lined with giant billboards, Broadway is still filled with people, even more so since 2009, when vehicles were banned from six blocks, welcoming pedestrians onto the roadway. But the scene was quite different in the 1960s when prostitutes, drug trafficking, and pornographic movies spread throughout the area, swallowing up or shutting down dozens of Broadway theaters. The survivors retreated to the side streets, but the sleaze followed. The neighborhood finally cast off its squalid past in the 1990s through a major investment of public and private funds that restored the theaters and brought in new office towers, hotels, megastores, and family attractions.

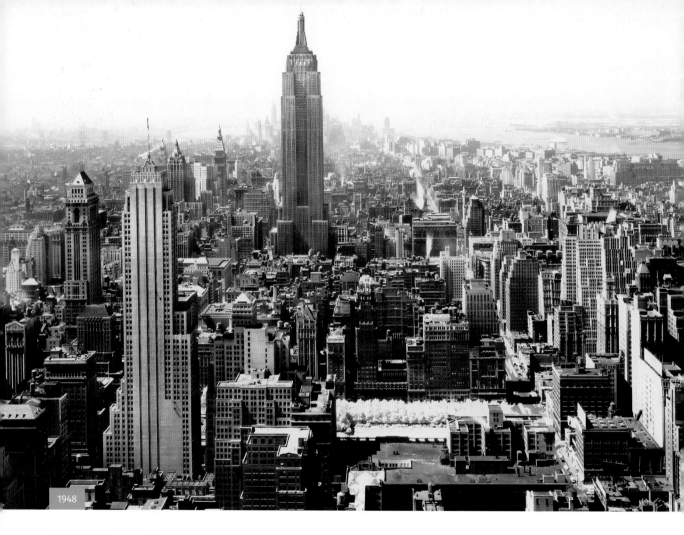

1948

MIDTOWN SKYLINE

Packed with skyscrapers by the middle of the twentieth
century, the city has grown even taller in the twenty-first

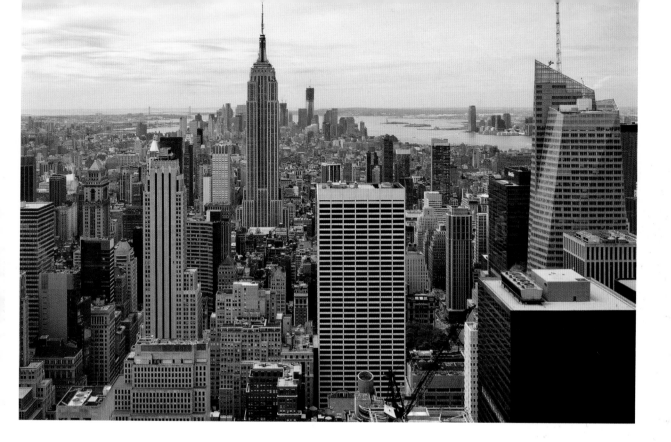

LEFT: Seen from the seventieth floor of the RCA Building in Rockefeller Center in 1948, this view to the south is dominated by the city's tallest structure, the Empire State Building. The tower in the left foreground at Fifth Avenue and Forty-second Street was a precursor to the Empire State. Both were built by the same architects, Shreve, Lamb and Harmon, just a year apart, in 1930 and 1931. The Empire State's original design called for a flat top, but the owners insisted on a distinctive spire as a mooring mast for dirigibles. Used only twice for that purpose, it became much better known for hosting *King Kong* (1933). The open space is Bryant Park on Forty-second Street.

ABOVE: This 2012 view from the Top of the Rock, the observation platform at Rockefeller Center, still shows the Empire State Building as the centerpiece. But far in the distance, just right of center, the city's tallest skyscraper, One World Trade Center, is shown rising where the Twin Towers once stood. In the right foreground, the building with the unusual angles and tall spire is the new Bank of America Tower. Completed in 2009 on Sixth Avenue and Forty-Second Street, it is the fourth-tallest building in the city. Across the Hudson River (right), New Jersey's waterfront was bare of towers in the older photo, but now has its own skyscrapers.

DELMONICO'S

The restaurant's fame as the epitome of fine
dining outlasted its operations

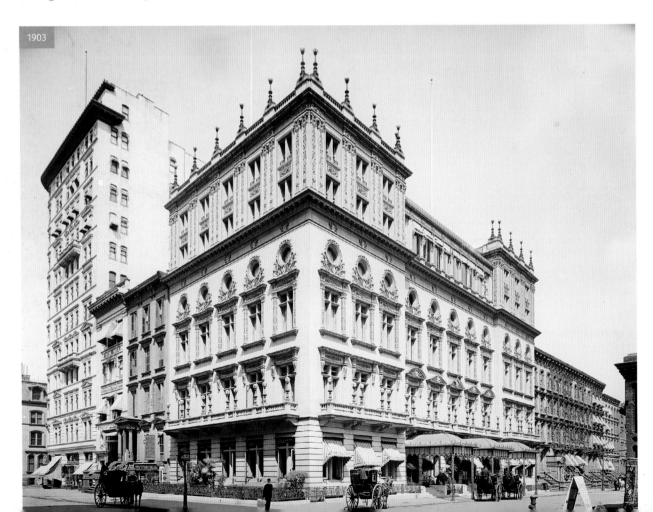

1903

LEFT: Synonymous with fine food, Delmonico's was the nation's best-known restaurant of the nineteenth century. By some accounts, it was the city's first actual restaurant, offering a bill of fare rather than a set meal like a tavern or an inn. The Swiss-born brothers Giovanni and Pietro Delmonico began the dynasty in 1825 as a small café and pastry shop in Lower Manhattan. The family expanded operations to six locations, each grander than the ones before, until opening at this elegant site in 1897. With sumptuous rooms on every floor, it drew universal praise—and surprise. Smoking, permitted previously only in the café, was allowed in the main restaurant. The change came in response to women who resented the fact that men retired to the smoking room after dinner. Another innovation was the addition of an orchestra to play in the background. Instead of quietly watching the performance, patrons could talk and enjoy such specialties as lobster Newberg and baked Alaska.

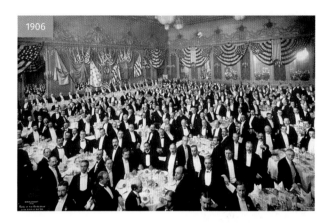

RIGHT: Although several restaurants around the country bear the name Delmonico's, the authentic family-run operation ended when the one at this site closed in 1923, just four years shy of a full century of distinctive dining. The end was the result of family disputes, changing customs after World War I, and, above all, Prohibition. Ironically, the last banquet served at the Fifth Avenue Delmonico's featured not champagne or fine wines, but mineral water. Delmonico descendants tried to prevent other restaurants from using their name, but a court ruled that once the family had abandoned the business, the name was up for grabs. In effect, Delmonico's truly became synonymous with fine dining and had passed into general usage. Amid the pharmacy supplies and antiques stores that replaced the last true Delmonico's, not even a whiff of its gourmet history remains.

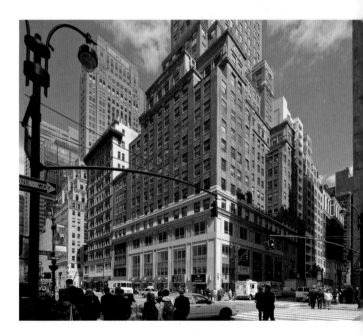

TOP RIGHT: The Sons of the Revolution attend their annual banquet. Delmonico's was the place where tuxedo-clad diners came together to celebrate their upper-class organizations.

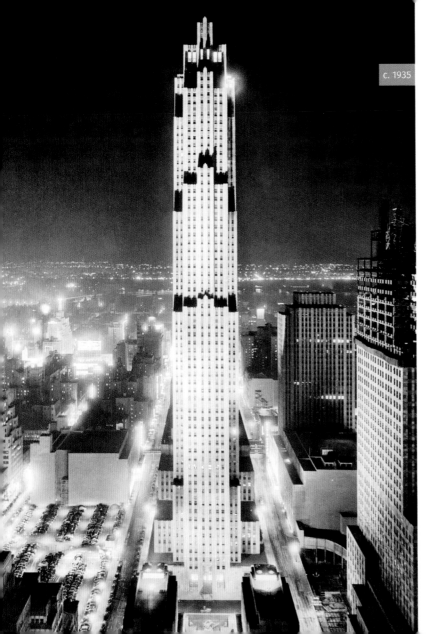

c. 1935

ROCKEFELLER CENTER

Designed as a home for opera, it became a center for radio and television networks

LEFT: Rising seventy stories in the midst of Rockefeller Center in this view is the just-completed RCA Building, the centerpiece of a vast development in Midtown Manhattan. Its size, undertaken during the worst years of the Great Depression, was mind-boggling, covering as much ground as thirteen Chrysler Building sites and providing as much office space as two Empire State Buildings. The project was advanced by two of the most powerful businessmen in the United States in the 1920s: John D. Rockefeller Jr., who inherited his father's Standard Oil fortune, and Owen Young, the chairman of General Electric. The project was conceived as a grand home for a new metropolitan opera house, but its immense commercial nature overwhelmed the opera's backers and they pulled out, giving GE and its radio networks, RCA and NBC, the starring roles.

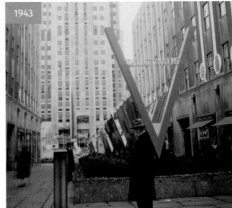

1943

RIGHT: Now Midtown's showcase, Rockefeller Center includes nineteen buildings between Fifth and Sixth Avenues and Forty-eighth and Fifty-first Streets—office towers, theaters, television studios, and restaurants, all connected to an underground shopping concourse and the famous plaza. The central tower, originally the RCA Building and now the GE Building, also known as 30 Rockefeller Center, is home to NBC Television Studios. The lobby walls were originally covered with murals by Diego Rivera, but were quickly repainted because the Rockefellers objected to the artist's Marxist imagery. An observation deck offering spectacular views from the seventieth floor was closed for many years, but reopened as the Top of the Rock in 2005.

LEFT: During World War II, a "V" for victory was installed in Rockefeller Center's Channel Gardens. The RCA Building is in the background.

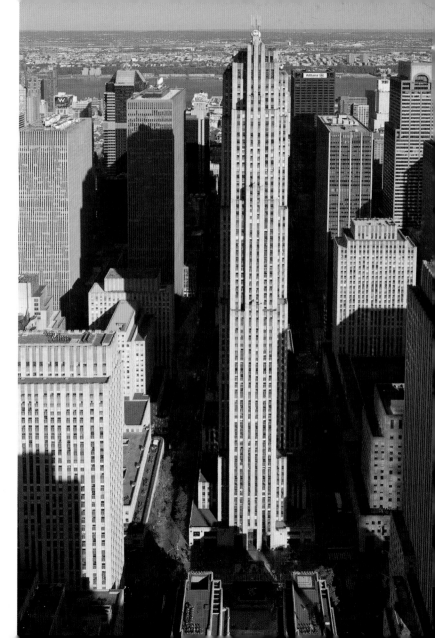

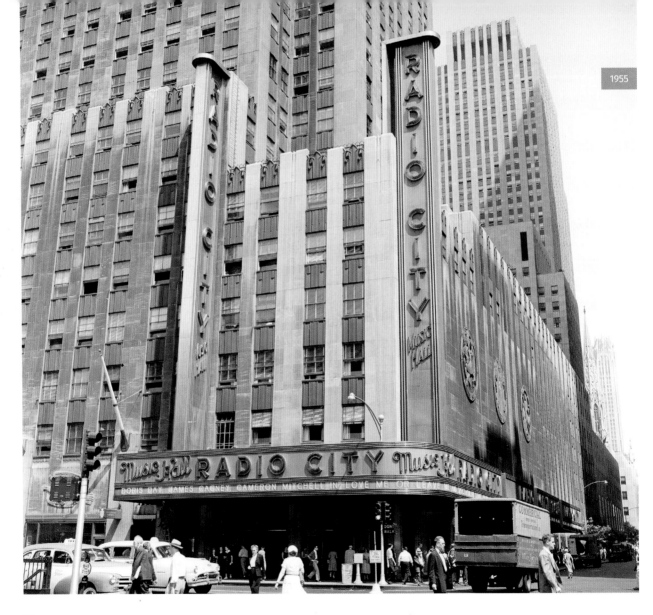

RADIO CITY

Once the largest theater in the world

LEFT: Radio City, the original name for Rockefeller Center, also included this grand music hall on Sixth Avenue and Fiftieth Street. With 6,200 seats, Radio City Music Hall was the largest theater in the world when it opened in 1932. It began exclusively as a vaudeville stage, but lost tens of thousands of dollars in its first two weeks of operation. It soon switched to movies, premiering *King Kong* in 1933. The combination of popular movies with live musical productions by the dancing Rockettes—originally called the Roxyettes after their first manager Samuel "Roxy" Rothafel—kept the theater going for decades. At the time of this 1955 view, it was the city's premier showplace for family films and entertainment.

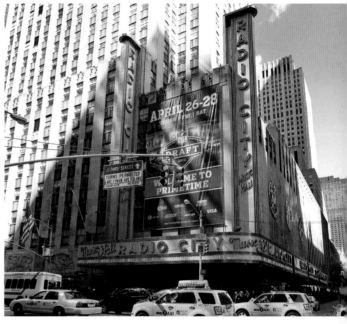

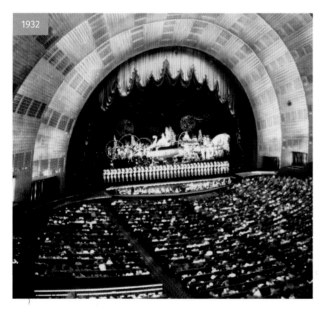

1932

ABOVE: By the 1970s, as the audience for family movies and stage shows declined, Radio City Music Hall was losing business again. In 1978, the city was shocked by an announcement that the theater, with its striking Art Deco interior and famous rising sun stage, would shut its doors forever and be torn down. Saved at the last moment by state support, it has been beautifully restored. Now managed by the operators of Madison Square Garden, it has switched back from movies to live concerts by a range of popular artists, from Cirque du Soleil to Lady Gaga. The Rockettes also return for the "Christmas Spectacular," kicking up their heels in sync as the long-legged troupe has done since 1932.

LEFT: The Rockettes perform at Radio City's opening night on December 27, 1932.

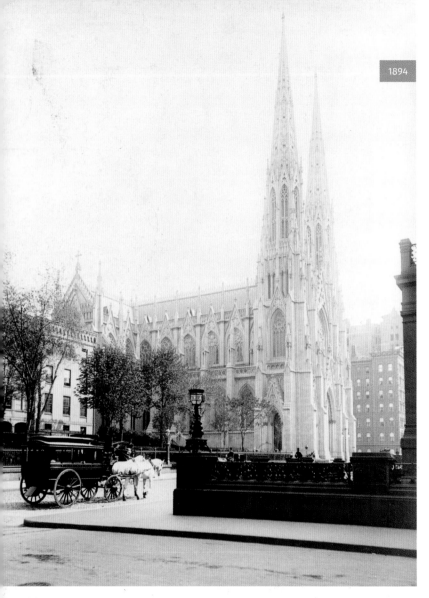

1894

ST. PATRICK'S CATHEDRAL

The magnificent building took thirty years to complete

LEFT: New York's Irish Catholic community was the city's largest immigrant group when construction of this grand cathedral on Fifth Avenue and Fiftieth Street began in 1858. Thousands contributed their nickels and dimes to make it possible, but a generation would pass before it was completed. Just two years after the foundation was laid, the work was interrupted by the Civil War and did not begin again until 1869. Although the cathedral opened to visitors in 1879, the twin spires required additional funds and were not finished until 1888. During this thirty-year construction period, the neighborhood surrounding the cathedral changed from a raw outpost to a wealthy enclave. The photo below shows Easter morning in front of St. Patrick's.

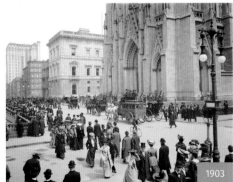

1903

RIGHT: New Yorkers and tourists of all faiths flock to St. Patrick's today. Recognized as one of the city's greatest buildings, it stands out as a unique architectural achievement among more modern structures. Rockefeller Center rose across Fifth Avenue in the 1930s. St. Patrick's glass-walled neighbor on the left is the Olympic Tower, built in 1976 as one of the city's first luxury condominium buildings, combining expensive apartments with offices and shops below. Many of the city's most solemn and festive occasions have taken place at the cathedral, from the funeral of the slain Robert F. Kennedy in 1968 to the annual St. Patrick's Day Parade on Fifth Avenue.

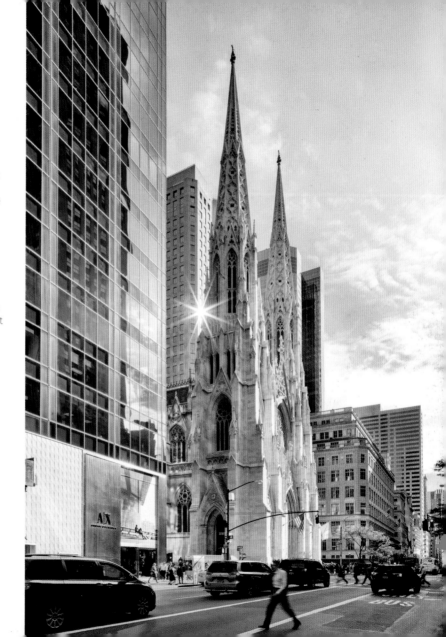

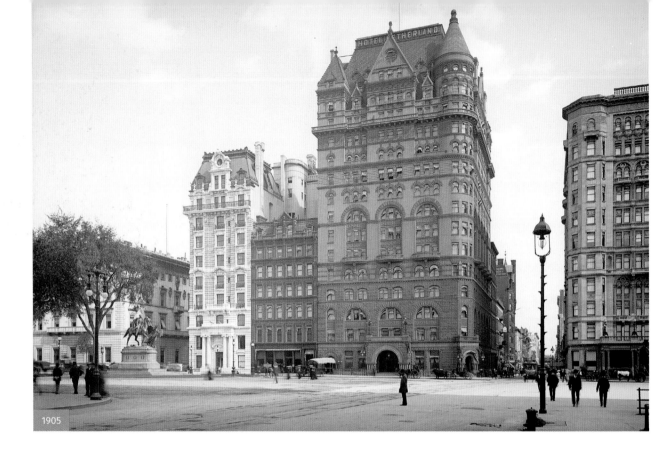

1905

FIFTH AVENUE AT FIFTY-NINTH STREET

A famous "skyscraper hotel" rose here at the entrance to Central Park

ABOVE: Fashionable hotels began to cluster around this site at the entrance to Central Park in the 1890s. The fifteen-story New Netherland Hotel, the tallest building shown here, went up in 1892. It was developed by William Waldorf Astor. On the far left is the Metropolitan Club, an Italian-style palazzo built in 1894 by the city's wealthiest and most prominent residents. This 1905 photo also shows the equestrian statue of the Civil War general William T. Sherman (left), erected in 1903. Critics objected to its placement here because they feared that the "skyscraper hotel" would dwarf the memorial.

BELOW: While the tower of the Sherry-Netherland was under construction, a fire broke out in the wooden scaffolding and enveloped the upper part of the building. Fire department pumps could not reach the top of the structure, and the water pipes in the building were not working yet. Crowds gathered in front of the hotel, and those who could afford it took rooms in the Plaza across the street to watch the spectacle. Fortunately, the fire burned itself out before doing any serious damage, and the Sherry-Netherland opened later that year.

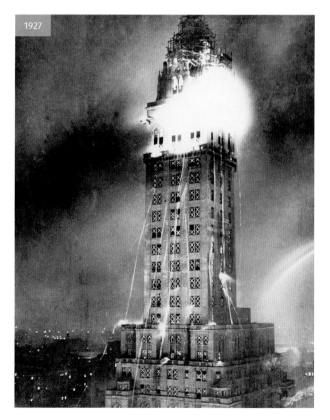

1927

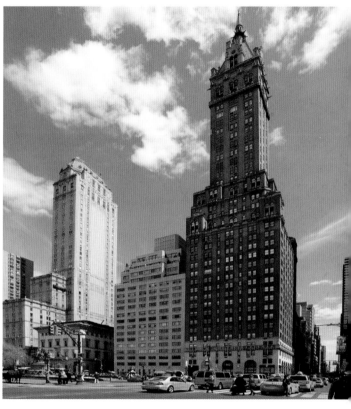

ABOVE: The Sherry-Netherland still has a commanding presence. Its distinctive tower sets it apart from other skyscrapers. The crown and pinnacle give it the appearance of a very tall French castle. Located across the street from Central Park, it offers stunning views and elegant accommodations. It was designed by Schulze and Weaver, the firm that created the new Waldorf-Astoria in 1931. The low-rise Metropolitan Club also still reigns as an elite club and impressive example of Gilded Age architecture on the park.

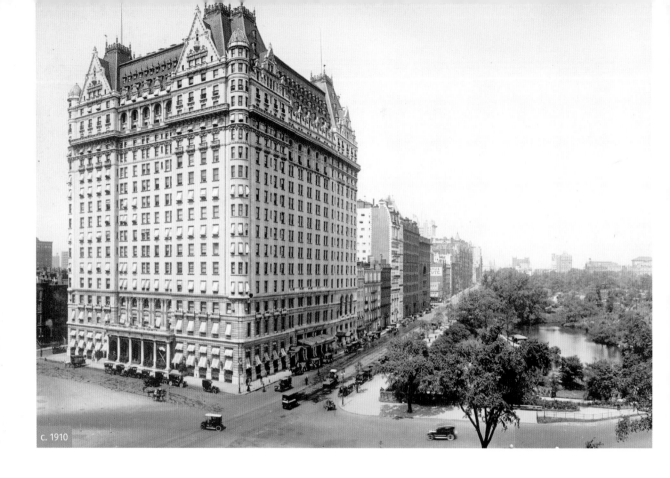

c. 1910

PLAZA HOTEL

Built in 1907, the Plaza became the most fashionable hotel of its day

ABOVE: By the turn of the twentieth century, this site at the Fifth Avenue and Fifty-ninth Street entrance to Central Park was the preeminent place for a luxury hotel. The first Plaza Hotel, a classical structure by architects McKim, Mead and White, was built here in 1893. But it was considered outdated by 1905. The new Plaza, built in 1907, soon eclipsed the Waldorf-Astoria as the most fashionable hotel of the day. It was here that American tycoons could follow the English lifestyle of living in country estates and spending the fashionable winter season in an elegant hotel.

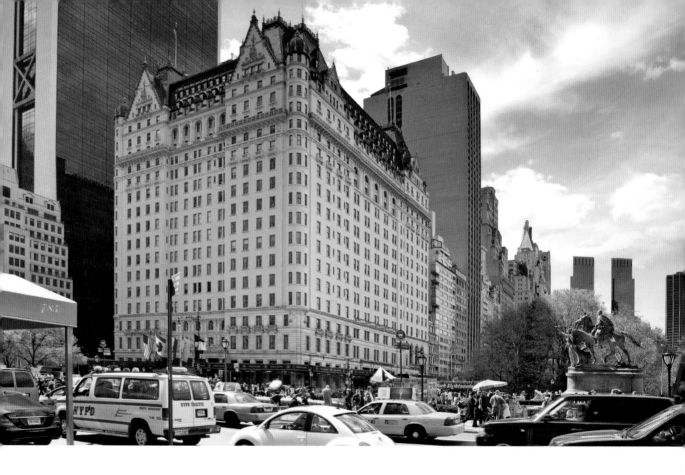

ABOVE: Recognized as a crown jewel at the head of Central Park, the Plaza Hotel was designated a city landmark in 1969. This prevented demolition, but a series of hotel owners had already altered the interior rooms, losing such splendid features as the Palm Court's Tiffany glass ceiling in 1943. By the late 1980s, the hotel's crown was noticeably tarnished. More owners, including Donald Trump, who refurbished the public rooms, came and went. In 2007, the year of its centennial, a new group of developers reopened the hotel with multimillion-dollar apartments.

FIFTH AVENUE AT EAST SIXTY-FIFTH STREET

Caroline Astor's Gilded Age mansion was replaced by the city's largest synagogue

BELOW: The château on the right facing Central Park is a double palace that provided ample room for Caroline Astor, her son John Jacob Astor IV, and on special occasions, the guests she deemed prominent enough to attend her annual balls. The self-crowned queen of New York society in the Gilded Age, Mrs. Astor was a descendant of the city's original Dutch settlers and famously compiled a list of "the four hundred" members of New York's social elite. Her move here in 1895 was a signal that the northern section of Fifth Avenue was the place to be. She held her last ball here in 1897. The photo on the right shows one of several elegant drawing rooms in the Astor mansion.

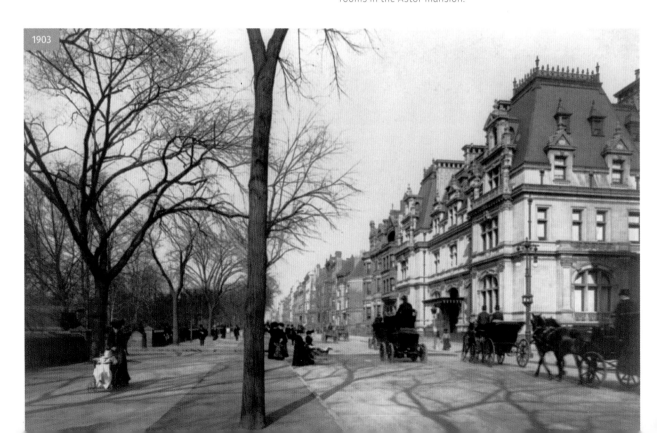

1903

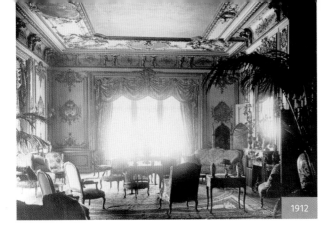

1912

BELOW: Astor and her son were supported throughout their lives by their family's wealth, which came in part from slum properties. She died in 1908 and her son perished when the *Titantic* sank in 1912. After their deaths, her grandson Vincent sold the slum properties and the Astor mansion and became a patron of civic causes. The mansion was demolished and replaced by this magnificent Romanesque Revival synagogue, Temple Emanu-El, in 1929. Its Reform Jewish congregation, the first in New York City, began in 1845 on the Lower East Side and has included notable New Yorkers such as Adolph Ochs, who transformed the *New York Times* into a profitable newspaper in 1896, and New York City former mayor Michael Bloomberg.

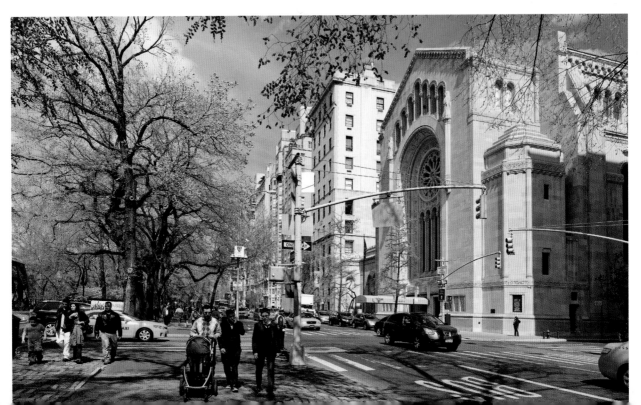

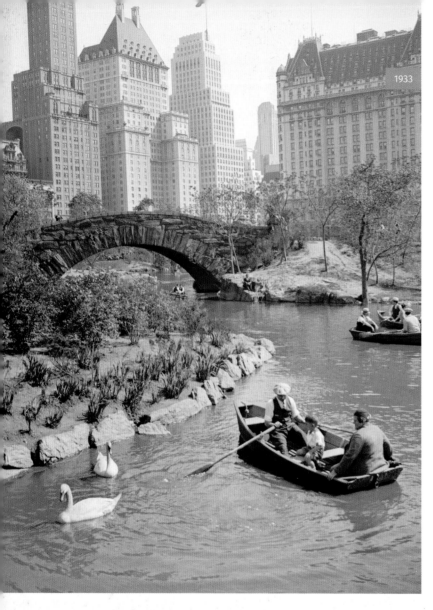

GAPSTOW BRIDGE, CENTRAL PARK

The rustic bridge and pond are a scenic foil for the surrounding city

LEFT: Just a few blocks inside Central Park is one of its most dramatic views. This 1933 photo looks southeast over the pond and Gapstow Bridge toward the Plaza Hotel on the right. On the left are two other luxury hotels, both built in 1927, the Sherry-Netherland and the Savoy-Plaza. The Gapstow in this photo is a rugged stone bridge that crosses the northern neck of the pond, near East Sixty-third Street. The photo below shows the original bridge, built in 1874 as a wooden structure with decorative cast-iron railings. The wooden arch did not last very long and was replaced in 1896 by the stone arch.

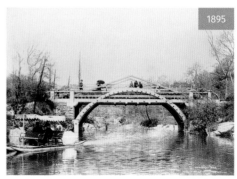

RIGHT: Like nearly all of the thirty-six bridges and arches in the park, the Gapstow is just as picturesque as when it was built more than a century ago. Although the park's designers, Frederick Law Olmsted and Calvert Vaux, expected the city to rise up around the park, they did not envision a backdrop of skyscrapers, certainly not the hulking General Motors Building that replaced the Savoy-Plaza in 1968. Yet to the modern eye, the contrast of the verdant landscape with the concrete-and-steel city makes the park even more appealing. Even though boats are no longer allowed on the pond, it is still a popular attraction, especially to the ducks who also enjoy the surrounding bird sanctuary.

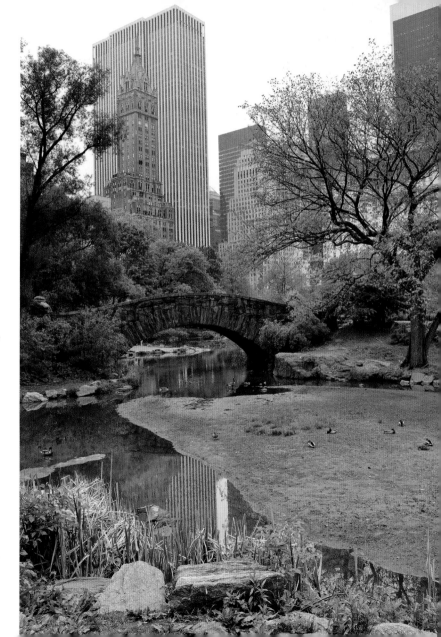

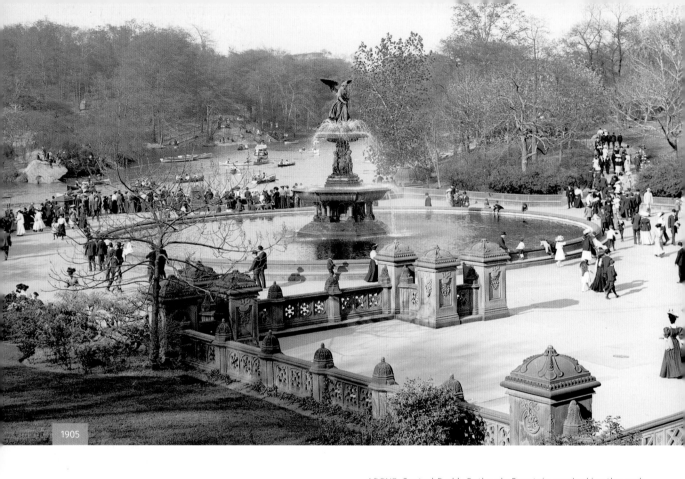

1905

BETHESDA FOUNTAIN

Originally marking the arrival of a clean water supply to the city, the fountain has become a symbol of Central Park

ABOVE: Central Park's Bethesda Fountain overlooking the park lake is one of the most scenic views found in the middle of a great American city. The fountain is topped by the winged "Angel of the Waters," which celebrates the clean water first brought to the city by the opening of the Croton Aqueduct in 1842. Sculptor Emma Stebbins was inspired by a Biblical passage describing an angel who bestowed healing powers on the pool of Bethesda in Jerusalem. The terrace and fountain, completed by 1873, were a park showpiece in this 1905 view.

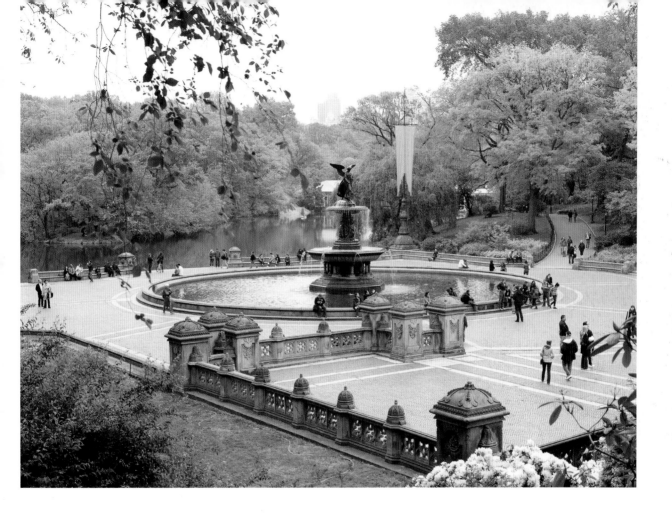

ABOVE: In the 1960s, the fountain became a hippie hangout, at times called "Freak Fountain." Physical abuse, made worse by continued neglect during the city's fiscal crisis of the 1970s, left the terrace scarred with graffiti, gouged carvings, and broken stairs. In the 1980s, the newly formed Central Park Conservancy raised funds to conduct a four-year restoration program, the beginning of a highly successful campaign to repair the entire park. Today, Bethesda Fountain, like the rest of Central Park, has been returned to its pristine glory. The statue of the angel, the most photographed monument in the park, was the inspiration for Tony Kushner's award-winning play *Angels in America*.

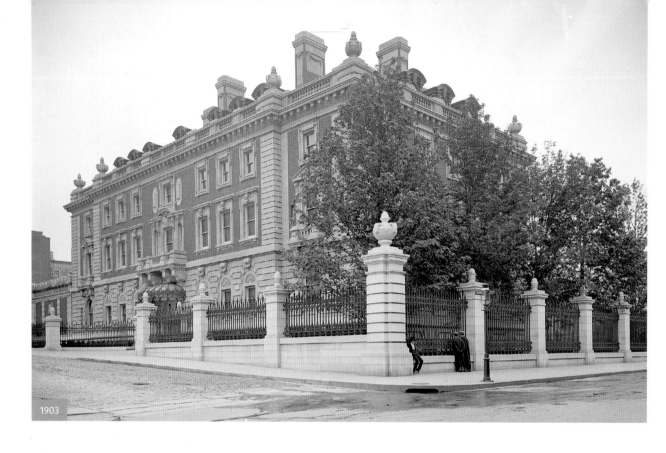

1903

CARNEGIE MANSION

Designed as a "modest" home for the Carnegie family, the mansion has become a museum

ABOVE: It may not look "modest and plain," but that was what steel magnate Andrew Carnegie told his architects to create when they designed this residence for his family in 1899. Considering what he could afford to build the house was not ostentatious, certainly not in comparison to the palaces of the Gilded Age. But it was huge, with sixty-four rooms, standing prominently in a large private garden along Fifth Avenue between Ninetieth and Ninety-first Streets. Yet, it was far from the fashionable part of Fifth Avenue. When the family moved into the house in 1901, the neighbors were squatters. Carnegie's former partner Henry Frick called Carnegie's home a "shack."

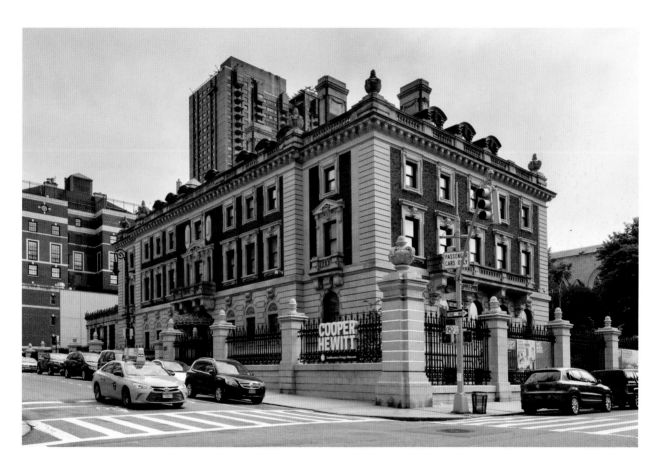

ABOVE: Carnegie's formerly unfashionable neighborhood is now the quite fashionable Carnegie Hill. His home, a few blocks north of the Metropolitan Museum of Art, is part of Museum Mile on upper Fifth Avenue. Carnegie's wife, Louise, lived in the house until her death in 1946. It became a city landmark in 1967 and in 1976 was converted to house the Cooper-Hewitt National Design Museum.

The granddaughters of another steel-rich philanthropist, Peter Cooper, established the museum in 1897 at Cooper Union. With ample room within Carnegie's spacious mansion, the museum has amassed 250,000 items, from ancient China to the present day. It is the only museum in the country focused solely on historic and contemporary design.

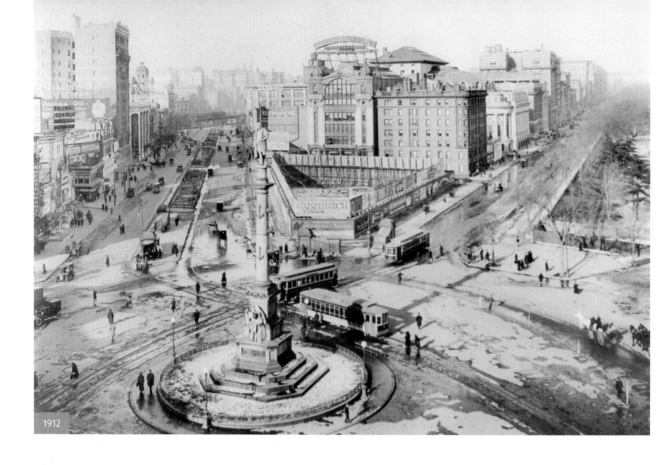

1912

COLUMBUS CIRCLE

Since the erection of the monument, its
surrounding neighborhood has been transformed

ABOVE: This intersection became known as Columbus Circle on
October 12, 1892. On that date, the 400th anniversary of Columbus's
landing in the New World, Italian Americans dedicated the marble
column in the center of the circle. Two years later, they topped it off
with the statue of Columbus. Broadway is on the left and Central
Park West is on the right. A corner of Central Park is shown on the
far right. The structure at the apex of the triangle was formerly an
equestrian school, being rebuilt here as an automobile showroom,
as seen by the "United States Motor Co," sign on top of the center
building.

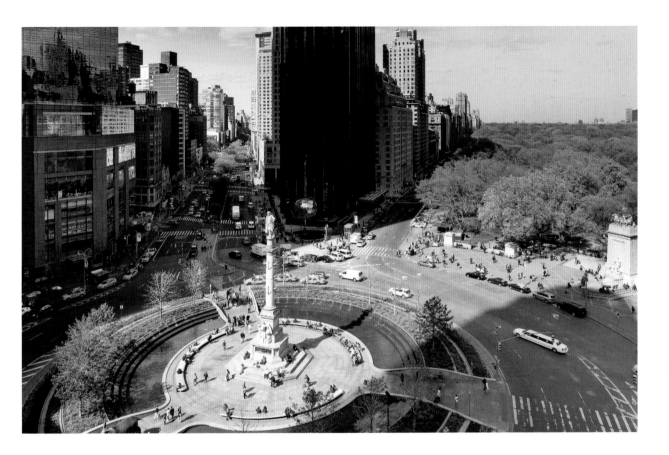

ABOVE: Except for the park trees and the Columbus Monument, everything in this view is dramatically different from the archival photo. Towering buildings now line all of the streets leading to the circle. The tower at the apex of Broadway and Central Park West went up in 1970 as the Gulf and Western Building. In 1996, it became the Trump International Hotel and Tower. On the left is the base of the Time Warner Center, a shopping, hotel, and entertainment complex built in 2003. No longer the cheap side of the park, Central Park West now rivals Fifth Avenue for high-priced living. Behind the Trump building, the towers at 15 Central Park West opened in 2007 as the city's most expensive housing development. The land alone, covering about one city block, sold for a record-breaking $401 million.

135

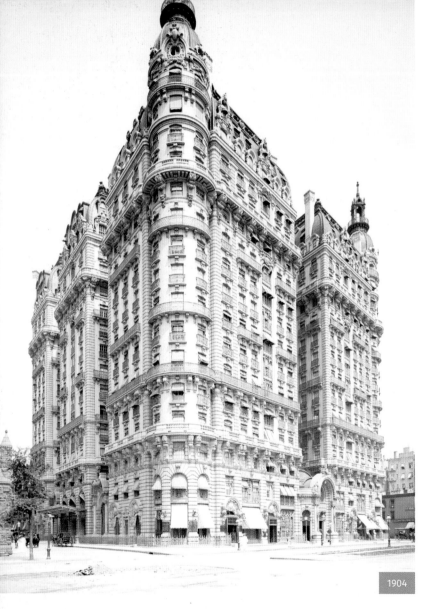

1904

ANSONIA

A lavish hotel with an eccentric history

LEFT: Built by the heir to the Phelps-Dodge copper fortune, W. E. D. Stokes, the Ansonia opened in 1904 as a lavish residential hotel on upper Broadway between West Seventy-third and Seventy-fourth Streets. Although not as fashionable as Fifth Avenue on Manhattan's East Side, the Upper West Side was attracting wealthy New Yorkers to the new trend of luxurious apartment living. The Ansonia apartments had multiple bedrooms, parlors, libraries, and formal dining rooms, served by central kitchens and professional chefs on each floor. The building was the first air-conditioned hotel in New York and also offered a ballroom, restaurants, and a lobby with live seals. Even more unusual, it had a small farm on the roof, a feature of Stokes's dream of self-sufficiency. A cattle elevator transported the dairy cows, and every morning a bellhop delivered fresh eggs to the residents. However, the dream of urban farming came to an end when the Department of Health shut down the farm in 1907.

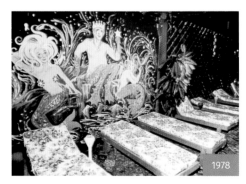

1978

RIGHT: The Ansonia was home to celebrated residents of the early twentieth century—from Jack Dempsey and Babe Ruth to musical legends Enrico Caruso, Igor Stravinsky, Arturo Toscanini, Lily Pons, and others who could play and sing within their thick-walled suites without disturbing the neighbors. By mid-century, most of the grand apartments had been divided into smaller units, but residents managed to fight off a proposal to demolish the building in the 1960s. During this time, the building's Turkish baths became an infamous gay club, the Continental Baths, where Bette Midler, accompanied by Barry Manilow, began her singing career. From 1977 to 1980, the baths switched to Plato's Retreat, a heterosexual swingers' club. The apartments were converted to condominiums in 1992, and by 2007, most of the buyers had reassembled clusters of units into the spacious apartments of the Ansonia's glory days.

LEFT: The lounge chairs and murals are part of the decor of Plato's Retreat, a sex club that operated in the hotel's Turkish baths from 1977 to 1980.

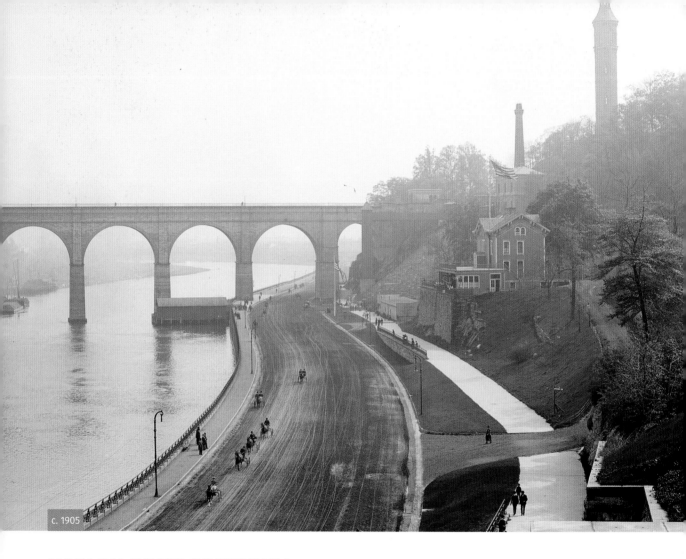
c. 1905

HARLEM RIVER SPEEDWAY

Passing under two scenic bridges, the speedway was an exclusive drive for wealthy carriage owners

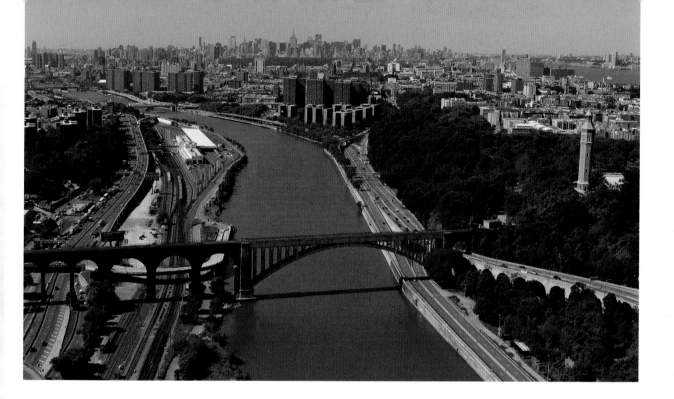

LEFT: This scenic stretch of the Harlem River in northern Manhattan opened to high-class horse-drawn vehicles in 1898. Commercial wagons were banned from the roadway, making it an exclusive drive for the wealthy, the only ones who could afford carriages. An elegant carriage could cost up to $1,200, four times the annual salary of an average New Yorker. Carriage riding was a favorite pastime of the leisure class, and the speedway provided a rare, unobstructed two-and-a-half-mile run. This view of the speedway looks south toward the Highbridge, completed in 1848 as an aqueduct carrying water to New York from the Croton watershed north of the city. The tower on the right, added in 1872, enclosed a water tank to serve the growing number of people living in the surrounding area. Since the area was at a higher elevation than the aqueduct, a pumping system carried the water into the tower.

ABOVE: Once automobiles began to traverse city streets, public pressure increased to open the speedway to general traffic. It was paved in 1922 and later became the Harlem River Drive (right). The Highbridge aqueduct is the city's oldest surviving bridge. Its masonry arches were removed in 1928 and replaced with a single steel arch to allow more room for ships. Its original pedestrian walkway, which had been closed since the 1970s, reopened in 2015 after a total restoration of the bridge. The tower no longer encloses a water tank, but is a historic landmark that can be entered on special tours.

SHEA STADIUM

Through thick and thin years for the Mets,
their fans came to the stadium

BELOW: Shea Stadium, the original home of the Mets baseball team, opened in 1964 and drew patrons from the adjacent World's Fair. It also hosted a full house of screaming Beatles fans for the group's famous concert in 1965. William Shea was honored for his role in creating the Mets in 1962, a team designed to replace the Brooklyn Dodgers, who left for Los Angeles in 1957. Although Shea Stadium in Queens never garnered the same affection as the Dodgers' beloved Ebbets Field in Brooklyn, the Mets embodied the Dodgers' underdog spirit and worked their way into the hearts of fans. After years of disappointing performances, the team became the Miracle Mets in 1969, winning the World Series. This view is from the walkway leading to the elevated station.

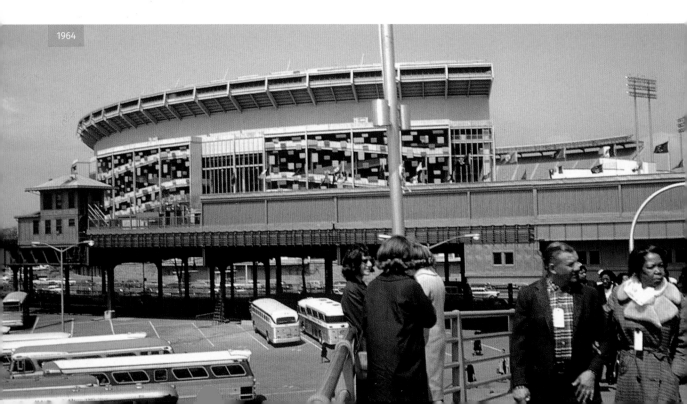

1964

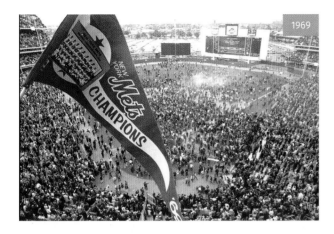

1969

LEFT: Fans stormed the field after the Mets' 1969 World Series victory, the team's first championship.

BELOW: The Mets won only one more championship at Shea, a dramatic victory over the Boston Red Sox in 1986, and finally made it to a "subway series" with the Yankees in 2000, a loss for the Mets but a riveting battle for fans throughout the city. Each team got a new stadium in 2009. As usual, the Yankees took the lead, getting the city to agree to share the enormous cost. Before the end of his term in 2001, Mayor Rudy Giuliani, a devoted Yankees fan, committed city funds for a substantial part of the new Yankee Stadium's controversial $1.3 billion cost. But the Mets did not lose out. To be fair, the city also built a new stadium for the Mets and paid a large share of the $850 million for Citi Field, named for Citigroup, which bought the naming rights. The new stadiums were built next door to the old ones.

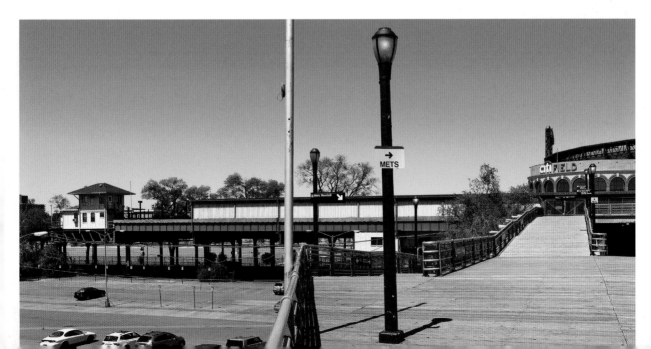

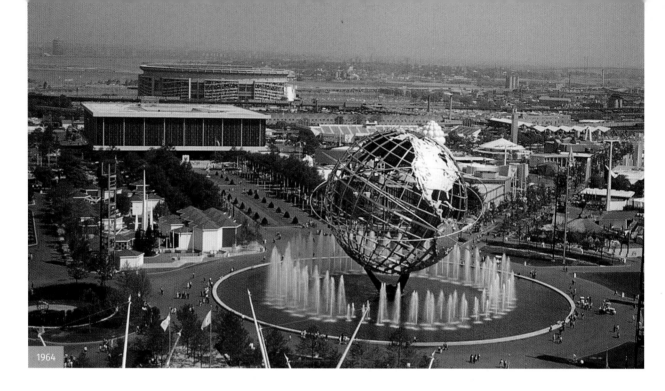

1964

NEW YORK WORLD'S FAIR

The Unisphere became the symbol of the 1964–1965 fair and a new icon for the city

ABOVE: From the Unisphere in the foreground to Shea Stadium in the background, this entire swath of land in Queens, nearly a square mile, was once a "valley of ashes," as F. Scott Fitzgerald described it in his 1925 novel *The Great Gatsby*. Literally an ash dump, it was transformed as the site of the 1939–1940 World's Fair, and had a second coming in New York as the 1964–1965 World's Fair, seen here. Gilmore Clarke, the landscape architect who designed most of the city parks built between the 1930s and the 1960s, laid out the geometric plans for both fairs. He also designed the Unisphere, the twelve-story-high steel representation of the Earth and orbiting satellites, celebrating the start of the Space Age.

RIGHT: The Ford Motors Pavilion was encircled by sixty-four pylons that rose above the building and curved inward. Critics joked that it deserved the "Venus Flytrap Award." But visitors enjoyed riding in 1964 Ford convertibles on the glass-enclosed "Magic Skyway" and gazing at Walt Disney's "time tunnel" of animated dioramas from the Dinosaur Age to "Space City." They tuned in to the narrations on their innovative push-button radios.

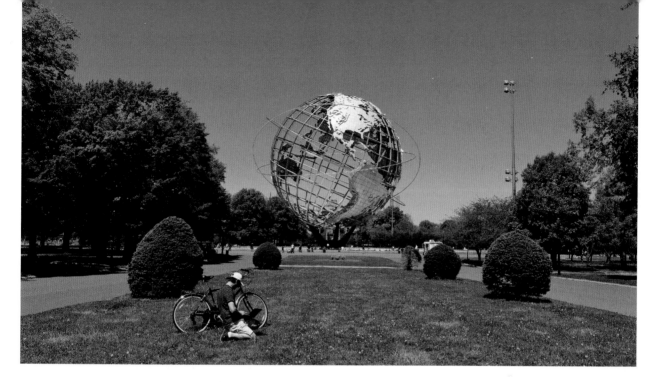

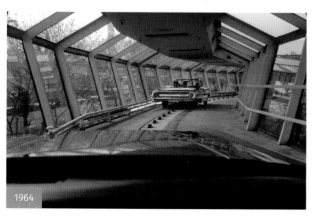

1964

ABOVE: Although the fair was a financial failure, it left a legacy. The site became Flushing Meadows–Corona Park, the second-largest park in the city. Most of the fair buildings in the older photo are gone, but today the park is filled with new recreation facilities, notably the National Tennis Center, host to the U.S. Open tennis championship, as well as new uses for some of the old buildings, including the New York Hall of Science and the Queens Museum of Art. The Unisphere, one of the few unchanged structures from the fair, was completely restored and has joined the ranks of New York City icons. In a reversal of the usual process, Manhattan followed Queens in adopting it. Donald Trump, a Queens native, had a smaller version installed in front of his Manhattan hotel at Columbus Circle. Some visitors, never making the trip to Queens, mistake it for the real thing.